The Golden Revolution

The Golden Revolution

HOW TO PREPARE FOR THE COMING
GLOBAL GOLD STANDARD

John Butler

WILEY

John Wiley & Sons, Inc.

Published by John Wiley & Sons, Inc., Hoboken, New Jersey.
Published simultaneously in Canada.

For general information on our other products and services or for technical support, please contact our Customer Care Department within the United States at (800) 762-2974, outside the United States at (317) 572-3993 or fax (317) 572-4002.

Wiley also publishes its books in a variety of electronic formats. Some content that appears in print may not be available in electronic books. For more information about Wiley products, visit our website at www.wiley.com.

Library of Congress Cataloging-in-Publication Data:

Butler, John.
    The golden revolution : how to prepare for the coming global gold standard /
John Butler.
        1 online resource.
    Includes index.
    Description based on print version record and CIP data provided by publisher; resource not viewed.
    ISBN 978-1-118-13648-5 (cloth); ISBN 978-1-118-23879-0 (ebk);
ISBN 978-1-118-26340-2 (ebk); ISBN 978-1-118-22531-8 (ebk)
    1. Gold standard.   2. Global Financial Crisis, 2008–2009.   I. Title.
    HG297
    332.4'222–dc23
                                                    2012003750

Printed in the United States of America

10   9   8   7   6   5   4   3   2   1

For those waiting patiently for the sunrise.

Contents

Acknowledgments

Few authors can claim to have written anything of value without obvious sources of inspiration and support along the way and I am no exception. Although not an academic, I do owe a debt to a handful of teachers who, in one way or another, taught me to think for myself rather than someone else or in support of an existing, defined paradigm. While this list could be rather long, I would particularly like to thank Miss Yvonne van Bronkel, and James Shipman.

At Occidental College, there were two professors who had a similar influence, Roger Boesche, and Larry Caldwell. Both were instrumental in fostering a desire to carry an intellectual approach toward life in my transition from academia out into the real world of business and finance, where I have now resided for two decades.

I received my first exposure to alternative, Austrian economics and the potential advantages of a gold standard system during a brief stint as an intern at the CATO Institute in Washington, DC. Although I did not know it at the time, what I learned while at CATO provided an important theoretical foundation for my eventual discovery that modern, fiat-currency finance, as I came to experience first-hand, was a deeply flawed, unstable system destined for some form of regime transformation. As such, I thank Christopher Layne, Edward Crane, and the late Bob Niskanen for the opportunity to work there.

No matter how brilliant a student's teachers or professors might be, there are certain things that can only ever be learned on the job. Thus, I would like to thank Richard McDermott, Sanjay Bijawat, Dieter Wermuth, Guido Barthels, John Wilson, Bhupinder Singh, and Wayne Felson for providing the opportunities that would allow me to continue my education while gainfully employed in the global financial industry.

With respect to the specific project of conceiving, researching and writing this book, I would like to thank Jeffory Morshead for encouraging me to start writing a regular newsletter, a useful warm-up exercise. Bill Bonner kindly introduced me to my publisher, John

Wiley and Sons. He has also provided an important influence on my understanding of the fundamental flaws of modern finance, and in a humorous way to boot. Thanks, Bill.

Friends and colleagues Jon Boylan and Julien Naginski provided not only moral support but also helpful comments on the manuscript. Betsy Hansen provided invaluable research assistance, including bringing a few obscure yet essential historical texts to my attention. Any remaining flaws or shortcomings of the book are, of course, entirely my own responsibility.

I must of course thank my lovely wife, Stephanie, and my four children, for tolerating my unusually frequent presence around the house while preparing the manuscript, and the inevitable domestic disruption that this caused from time to time.

Finally, I would like to dedicate this book to my late father, Kenneth Butler, who suspected, already in the early 1990s, that there was something wrong with modern finance. He struggled to put his finger on it but assumed that the exponential growth of financial derivatives, and the seemingly endless leverage they enabled, was symptomatic of something unsustainable. Little did he know that he was, in retrospect, amongst the first to identify the rapid growth of the so-called "shadow banking system" as a key enabling factor of a colossal future financial crisis, absent which this book would never have been written.

JOHN BUTLER
Bishops Stortford, England
March 2012

Introduction: Why a Gold Standard Lies in Our Near Future

> More and more people are asking if a gold standard will end the financial crisis in which we find ourselves. The question is not so much *if* it will help or *if* we will resort to gold, but when.
> —Congressman Ron Paul, Foreword to the Minority Report of the U.S. Gold Commission, July 1982

Contrary to the conventional wisdom of the current economic mainstream that the gold standard is but a quaint historical anachronism, there has been an unceasing effort by prominent individuals in the U.S. and also a handful of other countries to try and reestablish a gold standard ever since President Nixon abruptly ended gold convertibility in August 1971. The U.S. came particularly close to returning to a gold standard in the early 1980s. This was understandable following the disastrous stagflation of the 1970s and severe recession of 1979–82, at that time the deepest since WWII. Indeed, Ronald Reagan campaigned on a platform that he would seriously study the possibility of returning to gold if elected president.

Once successfully elected, he remained true to his word and appointed a Gold Commission to explore whether the U.S. should, and how it might, reinstate a formal link between gold and the dollar. While the Commission's majority concluded that a return to gold was both unnecessary and impractical—Fed Chairman Paul Volcker had successfully stabilized the dollar and brought inflation down dramatically by 1982—a minority found in favor of gold and published their own report, *The Case for Gold*, in 1982. Also around this time, in 1981, future Fed Chairman Alan Greenspan proposed the introduction of new U.S. Treasury bonds backed by gold as a sensible way to nudge the U.S. back toward an explicit gold link for the dollar at some point in future.

In the event, the once high-profile debate in the U.S. about whether or not to return to gold eventually faded into relative obscurity. With brief exceptions, consumer price inflation trended lower in the 1980s and 1990s, restoring confidence in the fiat dollar, which was particularly strong in the late 1990s. By the 2000s, economists were talking about the "great moderation" in both inflation and the volatility of business cycles. "Maestro" Alan Greenspan and his colleagues at the Fed and their counterparts in many central banks elsewhere in the world were admired for their apparent achievements.

We now know, of course, that this was all a mirage. The business cycle has returned with a vengeance with by far the deepest global recession since WWII, and the global financial system has been teetering on the edge of collapse off-and-on for several years. While consumer price inflation might be low in the developed economies of Europe, North America, and Japan, it has surged into the high single- or even double-digits in much of the developing world, including in China, India, and Brazil, now amongst the largest economies in the world.

The economic mainstream continues to struggle to understand just why they got it so wrong. They wonder how the U.S. housing market could have possibly crashed to an extent greater than occurred even in the Great Depression. They look for explanations in bank regulation and oversight, the growth of hedge-funds and the so-called "shadow banking system." Some look to global capital flows for an answer, for example, China's exchange rate policy and huge cumulative current account surplus. Where the mainstream generally fails to look, however, is at the current global monetary regime itself. Could it be that the fiat-dollar-centered global monetary system is inherently unstable? Is our predicament today possibly a long-term consequence of that fateful decision to "close the gold window" in 1971?

This book argues that it is. But it also goes farther. The global fiat-dollar reserve standard has now done so much damage to the global financial system that it is beyond repair. The current global monetary regime is approaching a transformation which will carry it in some way back onto some form of gold standard, in which monies, at least in official, international transactions, are linked to gold. This may seem a rather bold prediction, but it is not. The evidence has been accumulating for years and is now overwhelming.

Money can function as such only if there is sufficient trust in the monetary unit as a stable store of value. Lose this trust and that form of money will be abandoned, either suddenly in a crisis or gradually over time in favor of something else. History is replete with examples of Gresham's Law, which states in part that "bad" money drives "good" money out of circulation, that is, when faith in the stability of a type of money is lost, it may still be used in everyday transactions—in particular if it is the mandated legal tender—but not as a store of value. The "good" money is therefore hoarded as the superior store of value until such time as the "bad" money finally collapses entirely and a return to "good" money becomes possible. This monetary cycle, from good to bad to good again, has been a central feature of history.

Most societies like to believe that they are somehow superior to those elsewhere or that have come before, although it is only natural that this assumption is called into question during difficult economic times. But there are some laws to history and one of them is that money not linked to some form of physical standard—most often but not always metals—is doomed to a short, ignominious existence. The historical record is crystal clear on this. All purely fiat currencies eventually fall to their intrinsic value of zero.

Why should this be? Is not the story of civilization the story of progress? I believe that it is, but within certain limits, as provided by human nature. We may be civilized, but we are also human. All of us experience feelings of fear and greed at times in our lives, perhaps with respect to our basic needs, wants and desires or perhaps higher aspirations. There are those of us who might be overwhelmed by such feelings from time to time, those in power in particular, who tend consistently toward corruption over time regardless of whether they serve the public in a democracy or attempt to rule it in a dictatorship. One need look no farther than several modern, supposedly representative "democracies" now facing sovereign bankruptcy and default to see this potentially dark side of human nature in action.

To understand what is happening in the world of banking, finance, and economics today, please don't read an economics text-book full of equations or other mainstream, neo-Keynesian claptrap. Read history instead. It may not necessarily repeat but it certainly rhymes. We are deep into a crisis of monetary confidence from which there is no escape without a return, one way or another, to a metallic money standard. The evidence is there for those who care to look. But few are prepared to countenance that some of the more painful lessons of history must be re-learned in our time.

There has been much written about why the price of gold is moving higher and will continue to do so. It will, and probably much higher, when denominated in units of weakening fiat currencies. But, while this is certainly useful advice, it does not fully prepare the reader for the practical reality of the transition to the coming global gold standard, which is going to be substantially different from the fiat monetary and financial regime of today. It is not just money that is going to change. The nature and business of banking will change. So will finance in general. A gold standard will benefit certain industries, markets and countries but be potentially harmful to others. It follows that investment strategy and asset allocation methodologies must adapt.

A new global gold standard is coming. It is only a matter of time and how orderly or disorderly the transition is. Those who are prepared will prosper or at a minimum protect their wealth during the potentially rough transition period and be ready for what comes next. Those who don't may lose entire fortunes built up with the hard work of several generations. The stakes are high and they are real. It is time for us to leave the false comfort of our fantasy fiat currency "wealth" behind and get on with the business of practical preparation for the inevitable. And don't expect our so-called leaders or representatives in government to help. They are more likely to obstruct than assist in this critically important task.

This book is divided into three parts. Part I expands on the points made here regarding why the world is headed inexorably back onto some sort of gold standard. It explores just why the fiat-dollar standard was always potentially unstable and how the seeds of its demise were sowed many years ago, unseen by the economic mainstream. It then demonstrates how recent events, interpreted through the lens of economic and monetary history, imply that a return to gold is not only inevitable, but imminent.

Part II explores what the transition period might look like, including some historical examples of both orderly and disorderly monetary regime changes as well as provocative, hypothetical ones. History provides a rough guide for what to expect, to be sure, although we must give due consideration to the specific structure of contemporary international politics, including major geopolitical rivalries. In this section, we also consider how much the gold price is likely to rise as it becomes re-monetized.

Part III explores how the world of banking, finance, and investment will change under a future gold standard and which industries, countries and markets are likely to benefit and which are likely to suffer. Further, it looks at the implications for practical investment strategy and asset valuation. By fundamentally changing the very foundation of the global monetary order, the return to gold will affect interest and exchange rates, yield curves, corporate credit spreads, equity valuations, and the volatilities of all of the above.

The book concludes with a few thoughts on how the future gold standard will impact society more generally. It is my strong opinion that a world that has returned to a gold standard will be a far, far more pleasant, productive, peaceful, stable, and moral place than that which we for a time have allowed ourselves to be deluded into believing was, in certain respects, the best of all possible worlds. After all, they don't call particularly prosperous historical episodes "Golden Ages" for nothing.

PART
I

Why the Days of the Fiat Dollar Are Numbered

[T]hree-hundred and seventy-one grains of four sixteenth parts of pure, or four hundred and sixteen grains of standard silver.
—Original definition of a U.S. dollar,
1792 U.S. Coinage Act

This note is legal tender for all debts, public or private.
—Current definition of a U.S. dollar,
as stated on each Federal Reserve note

When one thinks of a reserve currency, one doesn't think of one that is exploding in supply, is backed by a central bank that apparently will stop at nothing to prevent an overleveraged economy from saving, is issued by a government running soaring budget deficits used to finance prolonged wars and open-ended welfare policies, is the legal tender for an opaque and quite possibly insolvent or even fraudulent financial system (e.g., the mortgage foreclosure fiasco, MF Global bankruptcy and apparent disappearance of supposedly segregated client funds), and has been chronically weak for nearly a decade versus not only other currencies but also precious metals, the traditional global monies. No, a reserve currency is naturally expected to be not only a reasonably stable store of value but also, arguably, the most stable store of value for the world at large; the anchor for all other currencies, be they officially pegged or allowed to float; and also the universal, benchmark unit of account for measuring wealth generally.

7

Of course, for most of the dollar's existence as the world's primary reserve currency, things looked quite different. In 1944, the United States was by far the largest, most dynamic economy in the world, with an industrial base bigger than the rest of the world put together. (Of course, much of the European and Japanese industrial base had been destroyed by 1944.) Victory in World War II was within sight, and the United States was emerging as the clear winner. Although both Britain and France were on the winning side as allies, their countries had suffered far more in terms of casualties, both military and civilian, and in terms of destroyed or damaged infrastructure. Both were essentially bankrupt and, without considerable U.S. assistance, were at risk of losing control over their long-held overseas empires (which they, in fact, did give up during the subsequent two decades).

The United States took advantage of this overwhelmingly dominant position and, in that year, negotiated the Bretton Woods arrangements (named after the New Hampshire town where the conference was held) between the victorious powers, with the notable exception of the Communist Soviet Union. Following a multi-decade period of global monetary mayhem, the ultimate cause of which was the economically devastating World War I, the United States took it upon itself to try to restore some degree of global monetary stability, in a way suited to U.S. interests, of course. It was generally accepted that a return to some form of gold standard was desirable, as it was believed responsible for the monetary stability that underpinned generally healthy global economic growth in the decades leading up to World War I, a period economic historians refer to as that of the classical gold standard. As such, the cornerstone of the Bretton Woods arrangements was that the dollar would become the global reserve currency, fixed to gold at $35 per troy ounce, and that other currencies would then be fixed to the dollar. It was a nice arrangement for the United States in that member countries' central banks were effectively forced to hold dollar reserves. This had the effect of lowering U.S. borrowing costs, a tremendous economic benefit not only for the U.S. government but for U.S. borrowers generally.[1]

---

[1] A study by consulting firm McKinsey in 2009 estimated that U.S. borrowing costs were some 0.5 to 0.6 percent lower as a result of the dollar's reserve currency status. See "An Exorbitant Privilege? Implications of Reserve Currencies for Competitiveness," McKinsey Discussion Paper, December 2009.

There was, however, a hitch, which was that by pegging the dollar to gold, in the event that other countries ran a persistent trade surplus with the United States—exporting more than they imported—then they would accumulate ever-growing dollar reserves. At some point, they might desire to exchange some of these dollars for gold at the official rate of $35 per ounce. Indeed, already in the 1950s, there was concern in France and, to a lesser extent, Germany, that the rate of dollar reserve accumulation was undesirable and unsustainable. But with the French franc and German mark fixed to the dollar, the persistent trade surplus required rising dollar reserve balances.

It was Charles de Gaulle, under the influence of legendary French economist Jacques Rueff, who decided in the 1960s to begin exchanging some of the accumulated French dollar reserves for gold. At this time, the United States held a huge portion of the world's gold reserves, and making gold transfers was not considered problematic. But as the years went by and the transfers grew in size, observers began to wonder whether the Bretton Woods arrangements were sustainable long-term. The United States held only so much gold. At some point, it might start to run out. What then?

A brief digression: Why exactly was the U.S. economy chronically losing gold to Europe? Well, by the 1960s, the United States was running chronic government deficits to finance a rapidly growing welfare state at home and wars, hot and cold, abroad. These deficits needed to be financed. Private domestic savings were insufficient to cover these deficits, so the savings needed to come from elsewhere, namely, Europe and, later on, also Japan. With foreigners supplying an ever-growing portion of the savings to the United States, their dollar reserve balances rose and rose.

Eventually, observers no longer needed to wonder where this was going. The market price of gold in London began to rise above $35 as global investors began to lose trust in the willingness of the United States to keep the dollar pegged there indefinitely. Gold was thus being hoarded into private savings as a way to protect wealth from the growing risk of a future dollar devaluation. There were coordinated attempts by central banks and governments in the late 1960s to hold the gold price down to $35 per ounce, but they failed under the growing demand for wealth protection. Finally, in 1971, the situation became untenable, and President Nixon made an executive decision to renege on the Bretton Woods arrangements and allow the dollar to float, that is, to decline theoretically without limit versus the market price of gold and, by corollary, versus any currency that chose to remain fixed to gold at the previous fixed rate. The fiat dollar as we know it today was born.

As for the future of the fiat dollar, to properly understand where we are going, it is necessary first to understand how we got here. As was the case under Bretton Woods, for most of its existence, the dollar was not a fiat currency. Indeed, for the greater part of its history, it was explicitly linked to gold, silver, or both in some way. While there is no specific reference to such a link in the Constitution of the United States, it was wholly unnecessary, as the circulating money of the time was overwhelmingly silver or gold coin, in particular the Spanish milled silver dollar.[2]

The Coinage Act of 1792 is the first instance of the U.S. Congress specifying an exact definition of a dollar, in this case, as a fixed weight of silver. The act also specified the value of the dollar as a fixed weight of gold by setting an official gold-to-silver ratio at 15 to 1, thus making bimetallism official federal policy. The act stipulated that the dollar would henceforth serve as the official unit of account for the federal government, as it does to this day.

Yet the definition of a dollar has changed radically since then. In the 180 years following the Coinage Act, as a result of one crisis or another, the dollar's explicit link to silver and gold was gradually weakened. President Lincoln temporarily went off the bimetallic standard, issuing so-called greenbacks to finance the Civil War. President Franklin D. Roosevelt nationalized gold holdings in 1933 and then devalued the dollar versus gold from $26.12 to $35 per ounce in 1934 in an unsuccessful attempt to end the Great Depression. It would be left to President Nixon, however, to sever the link to gold entirely, which he did in August 1971, inaugurating the era of the

---

[2]The history of the dollar long predates that of the Congressional definition in the 1792 Coinage Act. Indeed, the dollar was originally known as the *thaler* or *Joachimsthaler*, which translates into English as "from the Joachim Valley," which is in Bohemia, today part of the Czech Republic. Count Hieronymous Schlick, a Bohemian prince, minted the thalers in the sixteenth century. They were considered such a superior coinage that they became the standard by which other European coins were measured. The greatest coin minters in European history, the Spaniards, who brought back the bulk of the silver and gold bullion from the New World in the sixteenth to eighteenth centuries, named their benchmark coins *dollars*, after the fabled thaler. The term *pieces of eight* is also related to the thaler in that it refers to the fact that the Spanish dollar, when introduced, was worth eight Spanish reales, the previous standard Spanish coin.

unbacked, floating fiat dollar, with no official link to gold, which exists to the present day.

This part of the book explores the reasons behind Nixon's decision to close the gold window and the subsequent history of the fiat dollar, which, as we shall see, has been one of a steady series of crises, each progressively larger than that which came before it, and which collectively leave the U.S. and global economies on the weakest monetary foundation since at least 1933. By any reasonable measure, the fiat dollar has been an economic disaster that continues to unfold before our eyes. Fortunately, the days of the fiat dollar are numbered.

CHAPTER 1

The Window Closes

In the past seven years, there has been an average of one international monetary crisis every year. Now who gains from these crises? Not the workingman; not the investor; not the real producers of wealth. The gainers are the international money speculators. Because they thrive on crises, they help to create them.

—President Richard M. Nixon, August 15, 1971
speech suspending the dollar's gold convertibility

Treasury Secretary Connally was on vacation in Texas at the beginning of August 1971, when Treasury Undersecretary Paul Volcker requested his urgent return to Washington. A major global monetary crisis had been brewing for months, as one country after another sought to exchange some portion of its dollar reserves for gold, as was allowed under the Bretton Woods system of fixed exchange rates that had been in place since 1944. By July 1971, the U.S. gold reserve had fallen sharply, to under $10 billion, and at the rate things were going, it would be exhausted in weeks.

President Nixon entrusted Secretary Connally to coordinate economic, trade, and currency policy. Connally was thus tasked with organizing an emergency weekend meeting of Nixon's various economic and domestic policy advisers. At 2:30 P.M. on August 13, they gathered, in secret, at Camp David to decide how to respond to the incipient run on the dollar.

With the various attendees seated in the President's Lounge of Aspen Cabin, the president initiated the proceedings with a request that Volcker provide an update on recent events. The air of crisis grew thick as Volcker reported one country after another requesting to exchange dollar reserves for gold. Indeed, that very morning, the British had placed a request to exchange $3 billion in dollar reserves for gold. Something had to be done. Fast.

It quickly became clear that nearly all participants, including both Connally and Volcker, were in favor of suspending gold convertibility and floating the dollar versus other currencies. The primary dissenter was Arthur Burns, chairman of the Federal Reserve, who felt that almost any other action was preferable to abandoning the venerable gold standard that had provided the monetary foundation for more than a century of astonishing global economic development, including, of course, that of the United States. He also felt that suspending convertibility would send an obvious signal of U.S. economic weakness around the world, although, of course, this was precisely why there was an accelerating run on the dollar in the first place.

Rather, Burns favored dramatic policy action on the domestic front to restore global confidence in the dollar, including sharply higher interest rates if necessary. But everyone in the room knew that, were interest rates to spike higher, this would most probably cause a sharp recession, implying that Nixon was unlikely to be reelected the following year.[1]

In a final, desperate appeal to the emotions of those in the room who appeared to already have made up their minds, Burns claimed that "*Pravda* will headline this as a sign of the collapse of capitalism." Yet his objections, however passionate, were overruled by the other participants. The next day, notwithstanding a further consultation with Burns, the president made his decision to close the gold window, effectively ending the Bretton Woods era of fixed exchange rates by executive order.

On Monday, he announced the end of dollar convertibility as one of several bold measures—collectively termed the Nixon

[1] Burns's specific recommendations at Camp David may have been rejected, but the key aspects of his plan to restore confidence in the dollar, including sharply higher interest rates, anticipated the series of steps that future Fed Chairman Paul Volcker would take in 1979–1980, when another run on the dollar ensued.

Shock—intended to shore up a deteriorating U.S. economy. In doing so, he blamed the "international money speculators" for causing the series of monetary crises and claimed that, by suspending convertibility, the speculators would be "defeated."[2]

Contemporary observers of the time and historians to this day consider this speech to have been a major political success. Not only did it create the impression that the president was in charge of the situation but also it created a villain that no American could but love to hate: the international money speculator. But as with so many political speeches, it had little in common with the truth, as we shall see.

"Exorbitant Privilege": The Real Reason Why Bretton Woods Collapsed

The dollar has been a floating, fiat currency ever since Nixon's August 15, 1971 executive order closing the gold window. But while Nixon chose to blame speculators for the gold-backed dollar's demise, the truth is rather different. Bretton Woods did not collapse because of speculation—after all, it was primarily foreign governments, not speculators, that were draining the U.S. gold reserve— but because of unsustainable U.S. monetary and fiscal policies that had been in place since the early 1960s.

Beginning in 1961, Jacques Rueff, French economist and informal policy adviser to President Charles de Gaulle, published a series of papers predicting that a steadily deteriorating U.S. balance of payments position would eventually lead to a collapse of the Bretton Woods system of gold convertibility and fixed exchange rates to the dollar. As such, he recommended that the system be converted back into something more along the lines of the classical gold standard, in operation from 1880 to 1914, under which balance of payments deficits between countries were settled in gold.[3]

As Rueff explained it, the rapidly growing, export-oriented European economy of the late 1950s and early 1960s was accumulating dollar reserves at a rate that would invariably cause economically

---

[2] This account of the events immediately preceding Nixon's infamous suspension of convertibility on August 15, 1971, is provided with permission by Joanne Gowa, author of *Closing the Gold Window* (Ithaca, NY: Cornell University Press, 1983).

[3] Jacques Rueff compiled his essays into two major books on the topic of Bretton Woods: *The Age of Inflation* (1964) and *The Monetary Sin of the West* (1972).

destabilizing money and credit growth, leading to price inflation. The solution to this situation under the classical gold standard would have been straightforward: Countries running chronic trade surpluses would steadily accumulate foreign currency, which they would then periodically exchange for gold, thereby maintaining stable exchange rates and limiting domestic money and credit growth. Countries running chronic trade deficits, however, would have to provide the gold. In the event that gold reserves ran low, a country would be forced to raise interest rates to stem the outflow. By increasing the domestic savings rate and weakening domestic demand, the trade balance would swing from deficit into surplus, and, in time, the gold reserve would be replenished.

Under Bretton Woods, however, the balance of payments was not intended to be settled in gold but rather in dollars. This allowed the United States, in principle, to create as many dollars as required to purchase as many imports as desired, as these would be absorbed by the central banks of the exporting nations as reserves. As exchange rates were fixed, countries did not have the option of allowing their currencies to rise versus the dollar as a way to slow or reduce the growth of dollar reserves. Reserves would thus grow indefinitely. For the United States, this was akin to being given an unlimited line of credit by its trading partners.

French Finance Minister Valéry Giscard d'Estaing famously described this theoretical ability to print unlimited dollars for unlimited imports as an "exorbitant privilege." Of course, just because one has such a privilege does not mean that one will abuse it, but beginning in the 1960s, the United States began to do just that. Among other things, in the early 1960s, the United States:

- Was in process of building the interstate highway system, the world's largest construction project in history to that time.
- Entered and subsequently escalated a war in Southeast Asia, fought primarily in Vietnam.
- Dramatically increased domestic social welfare spending as part of President Lyndon Johnson's Great Society programs.

Although perhaps not so egregious by the modern standards of U.S. government budget deficits, taken together, these guns and butter projects led to a massive increase in the federal budget, which, in turn, stimulated global economic activity generally

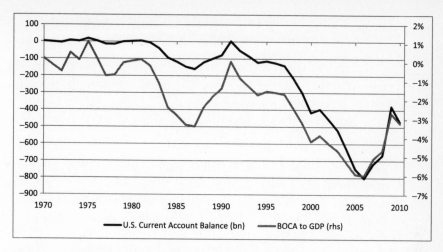

Figure 1.1   The U.S. Current Account Deficit through the Decades
Source: Federal Reserve.

and contributed to a substantial increase in the U.S. trade deficit (Figure 1.1).

As a direct result, dollar reserve balances around the world began to grow at an accelerated rate. Giscard d'Estaing was only one of many European government officials who expressed a sense of unfairness regarding the Bretton Woods system, not only in theory but also, increasingly, in practice. Indeed, even de Gaulle himself weighed in on the matter in a press conference in early February 1965 in which he stated:

> Any workable and acceptable international monetary system must not bear the stamp or control of any one country in particular.[4]

De Gaulle then pointed out that the only standard which fits this description is that of gold, which "has no nationality" and which, of course, has historically been regarded as the pre-eminent global currency. With the dropping of this bombshell, the formal European assault on Bretton Woods began. As *Time* magazine noted:

[4]As quoted in, "Money: De Gaulle v. the Dollar," *Time*, February 12, 1965.

Perhaps never before had a chief of state launched such an open assault on the monetary power of a friendly nation.[5]

This article was written more than six years prior to the proximate crisis that led Nixon to close the gold window. It is quite obvious that speculators were not behind d'Estaing's or de Gaulle's comments. Nor were they behind the following actions, as detailed in the same *Time* article:

- France converted $150 million into gold in January 1965 and announced plans for convert another $150 million.
- Although done quietly, rather than to the fanfare coming from France, Spain exchanged $60 million of its dollar reserves for gold.[6]

President Johnson responded to the accelerating drain of the U.S. gold reserve by easing the requirement that the Federal Reserve system hold a 25% gold backing for dollar deposits. While this no doubt bought some time, the die had been cast. Following de Gaulle's rhetorical barrage, the demise of Bretton Woods and of the gold-backed dollar, was probably inevitable. Perhaps, had U.S. politicians been willing or able to make some tough spending choices in the late 1960s, things might have been different. But Johnson, Nixon, and the dictates of domestic U.S. political expediency determined otherwise. In the end, as Nixon himself put it, it would take seven years and seven crises to finally sever of the gold-dollar link.

It is an interesting historical curiosity that, notwithstanding Rueff's prescience and de Gaulle's pontification, it was, in fact, West Germany that finally torpedoed Bretton Woods with a decision to allow the mark to float on May 11, 1971 (although it should be noted that this was done in consultation with France and other European Community member nations). In doing so, West Germany signaled in no uncertain terms to all countries around the world that the mark would henceforth be an alternative to the dollar as a reserve currency. The "gold-laden truckloads," as also noted in the *Time* article above, had been rolling for years. But it was not speculators at the wheel; rather, European governments had finally lost patience with inflationary, unsustainable U.S. fiscal and monetary policies.

[5] "Money: De Gaulle v. the Dollar," *Time*, February 12, 1965.
[6] "Money: De Gaulle v. the Dollar," *Time*, February 12, 1965.

In retrospect, it is clear that, the Bretton Woods regime was doomed to fail, as it was not compatible with domestic U.S. economic policy objectives which, from the mid-1960s onward, were increasingly inflationary. There is a clear parallel with today. The dollar remains the preeminent global reserve currency. The United States is also once again following highly inflationary policies, in an attempt to support the domestic economy following a massive, housing-related credit bust. Meanwhile, numerous economies, including the BRICs (Brazil, Russia, India, China), are experiencing high rates of domestic inflation as a direct consequence of U.S. economic policy, shifting their incentives away from a further accumulation of dollar reserves. As in the late 1960s, U.S. domestic economic objectives are taking precedence over global monetary arrangements, that is, the dollar's position as the preeminent reserve currency. It is only a matter of time before either U.S. policy must change or, alternatively, other countries must act to reduce their accumulated, inflationary U.S. dollar holdings. As such, today's regime has become unstable, although the monetary shoe is on the other foot this time round: It is other countries' domestic policy objectives—in particular their desire to maintain domestic economic and financial stability and contain inflation—that are in conflict with the current global monetary regime.

Closing the Gold Window as an Example of Global Monetary Regime Change

One theme of this book that reappears from time to time is monetary regime change. Nixon's closing of the gold window is an example of regime change. The dollar remained the world's reserve currency, but convertibility to gold was suspended. The definition of the dollar changed.

In this case, regime change became necessary because U.S. domestic political objectives came into conflict with its international obligations under the Bretton-Woods arrangements. The United States was unwilling to implement the more restrictive fiscal and monetary policies that would be required to stem the outflow of gold. Arthur Burns strongly preferred that course of action, believing it was in the long-term U.S. interest to maintain convertibility, but he was quite clearly outnumbered by Nixon's other advisers.

In her classic study on this episode, *Closing the Gold Window*, economic historian Joanne Gowa traces the origins of the debate that occurred and decisions that were taken in August 1971 at Camp David. What she finds is that there was a clear, long-held bias within the Nixon administration favoring domestic economic freedom of action over any international monetary constraints. When the two came into conflict, as they did when the gold reserves neared exhaustion, the former naturally won out over the latter.

As she argues in her book:

> From the perspective of politics within the United States, the single most important factor explaining the breakdown of Bretton Woods was the prevalence within the monetary regime's most powerful country of a nationalist outlook on the appropriate relationship between the United States and the international monetary system. In the view dominant within the United States, the international monetary system existed to serve the interests of the United States in maintaining both a healthy domestic economy and a foreign policy calculated to meet its security needs as it alone defined them. As a consequence, the monetary system would be supported only as long as it did not infringe more than marginally on U.S. autonomy—on the country's freedom to set domestic economic and foreign security policy independently of either's impact on the U.S. balance of payments or on the Bretton Wood's regime. Once that boundary was crossed, a withdrawal of U.S. support for the system was highly probable.
>
> The demise of the postwar monetary regime, then, can be attributed in part to the incompatibility that developed between its demands and the consensus that prevailed within the United States on the importance of regime maintenance relative to that

assigned to other objectives of the nation. The regime's survival depended upon a degree of subordination of national to internationally agreed upon goals; the consensus within the United States, however, implied a profound unwillingness to adjust national objectives in any significant way to the maintenance of an established network of economic interdependence. . . . That the incongruity would be resolved in favor of the nation's rather than the regime's priorities should not have come as a surprise to any observer familiar with the perspective that had long shaped the U.S. relationship to the Bretton Woods system. . . .

That the two did not collide irreconcilably before 1971 was a result partly of the noninflationary course U.S. domestic macroeconomic policy adhered to until the mid-1960s, partly of the vigorous demand for dollars abroad in the early years of the Bretton Woods system, and partly of the more recent series of ad hoc arrangements concluded between the United States and other governments to insulate the monetary system from the effects of a long series of U.S. payments deficits.[7]

[7]Joanne Gowa, *Closing the Gold Window* (Ithaca, NY: Cornell University Press, 1971), 103–107.

CHAPTER 2

Stagnation, Stagflation, and the Rise of "Darth" Volcker

When I look at the past year or two I am impressed myself by an intangible: the degree to which inflationary psychology has really changed. It's not that we didn't have it before, but I think people are acting on that expectation [of continued high inflation] much more firmly than they used to. That's important to us because it does produce, potentially and actually, paradoxical reactions to policy.

—Fed Chairman Paul Volcker
August 1979 FOMC meeting minutes

Being president of the United States was not easy in 1979. On the domestic front, although economic growth had been relatively weak on average for years, inflation seemed to trend steadily upward nonetheless. The OPEC member nations had, for the second time in a decade, demanded higher prices, contributing to that unfortunate (and, to Neo-Keynesian economists, perplexing) set of conditions now termed *stagflation*. New economic indicators were invented to help measure the malaise, most notably the Misery Index (Figure 2.1),[1] which simply added up the headline unemployment rate and

---

[1]Economist Arthur Okun created the Misery Index, originally using wage growth rather than consumer price inflation as a simple means to measure overall economic performance from the perspective of the average worker. It peaked at just under 22 percent in mid-1980, as Carter was running for reelection.

Figure 2.1   The Misery Index: Then, and Now
Source: Federal Reserve.

the consumer price inflation (CPI) rate. Having risen into mid-double digits by the mid-1970s, it was now rapidly approaching the 20s.[2]

On the foreign front, 53 Americans were taken hostage at the former U.S. Embassy in Tehran in November 1979, following the successful revolution of Ayatollah Khomeini and his clerical associates against the Shah, Reza Pahlavi (and the foreign powers thought to be behind him), in February. In Asia, there were occasional reports of sightings of American prisoners of war (POWs) in Vietnam, yet there seemed little the United States could do about it. Following its withdrawal some years earlier, the U.S. army had returned home, demoralized and, in the view of some, disgraced.

It must have seemed so unfair. Jimmy Carter, the 39th president, had inherited an economic mess. Exactly who was to blame was unclear, although as discussed in Chapter 1, the United States spent and borrowed its way into an economic crisis in the late 1960s and

[2]The calculation basis for the Misery Index has necessarily changed through the years as the methodologies for calculating the CPI and the unemployment rate have both changed substantially. Were one to calculate the CPI and unemployment rate today as they were in the 1970s, the Misery Index today would be far higher. For more detail on how this adjustment could be made, see economist John Williams's Internet site, *Shadow Government Statistics,* www.shadowstats.com.

early 1970s, and, taking the easy way out, President Nixon famously closed the gold window at the Federal Reserve in August 1971. Without the protection of the Bretton Woods system of fixed exchange rates, the dollar was now in full free float, and occasionally free fall, versus other major currencies.

Yet the dollar's weakness was not limited to currencies: Oil producers, previously selling oil at fixed prices in dollars, revolted against this devaluation in the denominator of the oil price by organizing supply and pricing conventions and forcing the nominator (i.e., the price) dramatically higher in the process. When Nixon told the American people on August 15, 1971, that allowing the dollar to devalue versus other currencies and gold would not be inflationary, he neglected to mention the obvious but unpleasant fact that U.S. trading partners in general, including the oil producers, would almost certainly raise their selling prices in response.

Almost overnight, OPEC became nearly as big a villain in American eyes as the Soviet Union. It was mooted in certain circles how the U.S. military, home from Vietnam, might be redeployed to deal with those Arabs—in so doing displaying traditional American geographical ignorance: Among major OPEC members, Iran is a Persian country; it may be Muslim but it is not Arab. And Venezuela and Indonesia are neither in the Middle East nor North Africa—the Arab part of the world—as those few Americans who did bother to look at a map might have noticed.

The demise of the gold-backed dollar and subsequent policy actions and reactions both at home and abroad all contributed to the harshest set of economic conditions the United States had faced since the 1930s. Sure, the United States was now an immensely wealthier country, with interstate highways stripping the landscape from coast to coast and (to paraphrase Herbert Hoover) not just one, but two or more automobiles in every garage.

Indeed, America was now so wealthy that a majority of young Americans were not merely graduating from high school but receiving some form of further education. Americans celebrated their wealth by consuming all sorts of goods and gadgets that had not even existed in any form but a generation earlier, such as televisions and all manner of home appliances. Leisure activities once reserved for the upper classes were now thoroughly middle-class pastimes, such as golf, tennis, sailing, and skiing.

Although the dollar had weakened since being allowed to float in 1971, it was still strong in purchasing power terms versus the rest of the world. Combined with the arrival of long-range, relatively cost-efficient jet travel, middle-class families could now contemplate foreign vacations, and those who did were amazed that they could eat fine French cuisine for the cost of an ordinary restaurant meal at home or stay in a grand hotel in many Old World cities for the cost of the local Holiday Inn.

The problem, however, as psychologists have learned, is that it is not the level but rather the change in our standard of living that matters when people consider whether they are satisfied with the economic state of affairs. We are wired to expect either stability or improvement: Any sense of outright economic decline, even from a lofty level, can raise dissatisfaction quickly, with obvious consequences for politicians.

Boldly optimistic on assuming office in 1977, Carter believed that he could use his salt-of-the-earth charm—he had been a successful peanut farmer before entering politics—to reach out to ordinary (voting) Americans and not just palliate their concerns but reinvigorate their spirit and shake America out of its national funk. In the epitome of this style, he began broadcasting regular fireside chats, in which he would wear a cardigan sweater in front of a modest, slow-burning fire, implicit signals to Americans that there were simple, commonsense ways to deal with higher energy prices. Once seated comfortably, he would inform his audience of what was going well, what could be improved, and how lucky they were to be citizens of such a fine country.

But perhaps like all peoples, Americans might enjoy listening to promises and platitudes, but what they really want are results. They were promised victory in Vietnam. They got defeat. They were promised a Great Society. They got civil strife and budget deficits. They were promised wage-and-price controls. They got a weaker dollar and inflation. They were promised the American dream. And they felt they were slipping into a nightmare. It might not have been Carter's fault, but the consequences of closing the gold window were showing up on his watch.

As the economy continued to get worse, Carter found that he had an unusually short honeymoon period with the electorate. But optimism gave way not to pessimism but to determination. He seized the opportunity to mediate peace talks between Egypt and Israel, eventually presiding over the Camp David accords, which would contribute to the decision to award him the Nobel Peace Prize in 2002. He embraced efforts to deregulate certain industries, such as railroads, airlines, and communications. He even made a push to provide comprehensive health care for all Americans but failed to convince Congress to go along.

Perhaps most important of all, Carter faced down the financial markets and set about repairing the economic damage unleashed in the aftermath of the breakdown of the Bretton Woods system.

The Rise of "Darth" Volcker

In the summer of 1979, as he approached the end of his first term and began campaigning for his second, Carter had a choice to make, certainly one of the most difficult decisions he would ever make. Inflation was rising. The dollar was falling. Unemployment was high, and it looked like the economy was beginning to weaken. The choice in question was whom Carter was going to appoint to be the new chairman of the Federal Reserve when the seat was abruptly vacated by Bill Miller, who left to head up the Treasury. The candidates included David Rockefeller, arguably the most powerful banker on Wall Street. But he declined, citing his prominent position and the public image problems it might create for the president. In his place, he recommended his onetime colleague and friend, Paul Volcker, who, incidentally, had been a key player in President Nixon's economic policy team and in the policy debates that culminated in the August 1971 Camp David meeting at which it was decided to end the dollar's convertibility into gold.

Notwithstanding Volcker's long tenure in various economic policy roles, the problem with Volcker, according to some of Carter's senior advisers, was that he was perhaps too independent; in other words, he was a noted hard money advocate who would not cave to pressure from the president or anyone else. He might not be enough of a team player. But Carter overrode his advisers, sensing that the best way to deal with an economic crisis was to bring in a tough guy with market credibility who, hopefully, would shore up White House economic credentials generally.

Carter could have done like some presidents before him, including Nixon, and deliberately given the economy a jolt of stimulus heading into the re-election campaign, boosting job prospects and carrying him through to a second term, but instead he did what he thought was best for the country, which was to tackle the problems before him right there and then, although he knew it could cost him the election. He overruled his advisors and appointed Volcker. And he lost to Reagan in a landslide.[3]

Paul Volcker was not just known as perhaps the tallest man on Wall Street. He had a solid reputation both as a banker and as a public servant. Notwithstanding a stellar career at the Chase Manhattan Bank, at the Treasury, and at the Federal Reserve Bank of New York, he was not particularly wealthy by Wall Street standards. He eschewed luxury. As one example, he commuted on foot, briefcase in hand, from a relatively modest apartment to his New York Fed office in Maiden Lane. Yet his legendary support for tight monetary policy would soon earn him the nickname "Darth" Volcker.

Following his appointment, Volcker didn't waste any time. At his first Federal Reserve Board meeting as chairman in August 1979, Volcker asked around the room for comments on the current state of the economy, what the Fed should be watching, and whether a change in policy was appropriate.

His board of governors colleagues and a handful of senior staff subsequently chimed in with a great deal of comment on the state of industrial production, inventories, employment, exports and imports, and all manner of economic activity. The general message was that the economy appeared to have entered a recession, although to what extent and for what duration was, naturally, unclear. But in keeping with the conundrum of those times, there was also reference to stubbornly high inflation notwithstanding persistent economic weakness.

Once the discussion had completed an initial circuit around the room in this fashion, Volcker weighed in, invoking a dramatic change

---

[3] It has been claimed, based on Carter's initial press conference following Volcker's appointment, that the president was not particularly aware of what Volcker planned to do at the Fed and appointed him in the expectation that he would provide continuity rather than an abrupt change in policy. While this is possible, it seems not plausible that a president clearly in the midst of an economic crisis, who has just announced a major cabinet reshuffle, would prefer continuity over change, rhetoric notwithstanding. In Volcker's own account, he stressed the need for tighter policy and strict Fed independence in his meetings with Carter prior to his appointment. For a thorough account of how Carter came to appoint Volcker to the chairmanship, see Joseph B. Treaster, *Paul Volcker: The Making of a Financial Legend* (Hoboken, NJ: John Wiley & Sons, 2004).

in subject and tone. Rather than talk about economic activity in any detail or anything remotely quantifiable, he focused on the more basic, qualitative issues of confidence, credibility, psychology, and symbolism:

> . . . This is a meeting that is perhaps of more than usual symbolic importance if nothing else. And sometimes symbols are important. . . .
>
> In general, I don't think I have to go into all the dilemmas and difficulties we face for economic policy. It looks as though we're in a recession; I suppose we have to consider that the recession could be worse than the staff's projections suggest at this time. . . .
>
> **When I look at the past year or two I am impressed myself by an intangible: the degree to which inflationary psychology has really changed. It's not that we didn't have it before, but I think people are acting on that expectation [of continued high inflation] much more firmly than they used to. That's important to us because it does produce, potentially and actually, paradoxical reactions to policy.**
>
> Put those two things together and I think we are in something of a box—a box that says that the ordinary response one expects to easing actions may not work, although there would be differences of judgment on that. They won't work if they're interpreted as inflationary; and much of the stimulus will come out in prices rather than activity. . . .
>
> I think there is some evidence, for instance—if a tightening action is interpreted as a responsible action and if one thinks long-term interest rates are important—that long-term rates tend to move favorably. The dollar externally obviously adds to the dilemma and makes it kind of a "trilemma." **Nobody knows what is going to happen to the dollar but I do think it's fair to say that the psychology is extremely tender.** . . . I'm not terrified over the idea of some decline in the average weighted exchange rate of the dollar or some similar measure. The danger is, however, that once the market begins moving, it tends to move in a cumulative way and feeds back on psychology and we will get a kind of cascading decline, which I don't think is helpful. In fact, it's decidedly unhelpful to both our inflation prospects and business prospects. . . .

In terms of our own policy and our approach, I do have the feeling—I don't know whether other people share it or not—that **economic policy in general has a kind of crisis of credibility, and we're not entirely exempt from that. There is a similar question or a feeling of uncertainty about our own credentials**. So when I think of strategy, I do believe that we have to give some attention to whether we have the capability, within the narrow limits perhaps in which we can operate, of turning expectations and sentiment. I am thinking particularly on the inflationary side. . . .

Specifically, that suggests that **we may have to be particularly sensitive to some of the things that are looked at in the short run, such as the [monetary] aggregates and the external value of the dollar. When we're sensitive to those things, there's certainly a perceived risk of aggravating the recession . . . it would be very nice if in some sense we could restore our own credentials and [the credibility] of economic policy in general on the inflation issue**.

To the extent we can achieve that, I do think we will buy some flexibility in the future. . . . If we're going to be in a recession, by all traditional standards the money supply does tend to be a little weak and interest rates go down. I suspect that's a pretty manageable proposition for us if long-term expectations are not upset at the time by any decline in interest rates—an action we might actually have to take to or want to take to support the money supply. But I don't think that approach will be a very happy one unless people are pretty confident about our long-term intentions. That's the credibility problem. . . .

I don't know what the chances are of changing these perceptions in a limited period of time. But as I look at it, I don't know that we have any alternative other than to try. . . .

In saying all that, I don't think that monetary policy is the only instrument we have either. I might say that my own bias is, while I certainly think in the particular situation we find ourselves it's premature to be arguing for a big fiscal policy move, that such a move might be necessary. If it is necessary, it ought to be through the tax side and it ought to be through a tax program that not only deals with the short-run situation but fits into the long-term objectives. . . . Ordinarily I tend to think that we ought to keep our ammunition reserved as much as possible for more of a crisis situation where we have a rather clear public backing for whatever drastic action we take. But I'm also fairly persuaded at the moment that some gesture, in a framework in which we don't have a lot of room, might be a very useful prophylactic—if I can put it that way—and would save us a lot of grief later. If we can achieve a little credibility both in the exchange markets and with respect to the [monetary] aggregates now, we can buy the flexibility later.

So, in a tactical sense, that leads me to the feeling that some small move now—I'm not talking about anything big—together with a relatively restrained [monetary] aggregate specification might be desirable. . . .

I might only say that I'm somewhat allergic to the use of the discount [rate] as pure symbol—in other words move the discount rate and do nothing else because I think there's already some flavor of that in market thinking. We do that about once and that means the symbol is pretty much destroyed for the future. (Emphasis added.)[4]

This meeting represents a turning point in U.S. monetary policy. In subsequent meetings, Volcker worked toward building a consensus around the idea, initially laid out in these remarks, that the Fed needed to communicate in a fundamentally different way with the financial markets. Given that the stagflationary 1970s had seriously undermined the Keynesian economic concept of the Phillips curve,[5] in which there was a quantifiable and manageable trade-off between unemployment and inflation, Volcker aimed for a clean break, and in short order he got it. To anchor inflation expectations, Fed policy itself needed an anchor. In October 1979, the Fed announced that,

[4]FOMC meeting transcript, August 1979, 20–23, available online at www .federalreserve.gov/monetarypolicy/files/FOMC19790814meeting.pdf.
[5]Although long associated with Keynesian theory, economist William Phillips did not publish his paper claiming that there was a quantifiable trade-off between wages (inflation) and unemployment until 1958. Although discredited during the 1970s, several modified, neo-Keynesian versions of the concept live on today, including the NAIRU, or nonaccelerating inflation rate of unemployment, and Gordon's triangle model.

going forward, it would target growth rates in monetary aggregates, which were believed to be consistent with low and stable inflation. The Phillips curve was out. Unemployment had been relegated *de facto* to a second-order priority. But the financial markets were not convinced. They would first have to test the Fed's new regime to see just how credible it was.

Their opportunity was not long in coming. In early 1980, notwithstanding a weakening economy, money growth remained surprisingly strong. The Fed, in line with its new policy, pushed interest rates higher and higher. The economy now began to weaken dramatically. Unemployment soared.[6] But Volcker was relentless. His priority, to restore credibility in the Fed and the dollar specifically and, by implication, in the U.S. economy generally, remained unchanged. Recession be damned; the Fed kept on tightening. At the peak, interest rates reached 20 percent (Figure 2.2).

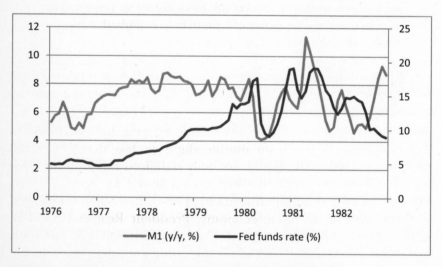

Figure 2.2   U.S. Money Growth and Fed Funds 1976 to 1982: The High Cost of Restoring Confidence

Source: Federal Reserve.

[6]Those who follow U.S. economic statistics closely are aware that the Bureau of Labor Statistics changed the definition of the so-called headline unemployment rate in 1994, from what is known today as U5 to U3, removing "discouraged workers" from the calculation. On either measure, unemployment today is comparable in magnitude to the peak reached in 1982.

The reaction on Capitol Hill was predictable. In one instance in the summer of 1981, when Volcker was answering questions before a Congressional committee, he explained that, notwithstanding the recession, rates were going to remain high as long as money growth failed to slow toward the targeted level. Vitriol followed:

> The Congressmen literally shrieked. Frank Annunzio, a Democrat from Illinois, shouted and pounded his desk. "Your course of action is wrong," he yelled, his voice breaking with emotion. "It must be wrong. There isn't anybody who says you're right." Volcker's high interest rates were "destroying the small businessman," decried George Hansen, a Republican from Idaho. "We're destroying Middle America," Representative Hansen said. "We're destroying the American Dream." Representative Henry B. Gonzalez, a Democrat from Texas, called for Volcker's impeachment, saying he had permitted big banks to be "predatory dinosaurs that suck up billions of dollars in resources" to support mergers while doing little to help neighborhood stores and workshops and the average American consumer.[7]

The Aftermath

Although Volcker's policies no doubt contributed directly to the most severe recession since World War II, he achieved his goals. Inflation plummeted from double digits to less than 3 percent by the mid-1980s. The dollar not only stabilized but also, by 1984, had recovered its 1970s decline (as measured in trade-weighted terms versus other major currencies). The United States reemerged as a productive, dynamic economy. President Reagan basked in this success, which he termed "Morning in America" and was reelected in a landslide. Yet when the going got tough again in the late 1980s and the dollar was once again in sharp decline, Volcker had left the stage, replaced by Alan Greenspan. The rest is history. A history of asset bubbles and financial bailouts. It is to that we now turn.

[7]Joseph B. Treaster, *Paul Volcker: The Making of a Financial Legend* (Hoboken, NJ: John Wiley & Sons, 2004), 5.

A Brief Introduction to Neo- and New-Keynesian Economics

This book makes occasional reference to Neo- or New-Keynesian economics, the dominant schools of thought represented by the economic mainstream today. The vast bulk of tenured economics professors and central bank research staff are members of these schools, which trace their roots back to John Maynard Keynes, who postulated that government deficit spending was an essential policy tool that could be used to moderate economic downturns, in particular those associated with weak or insolvent financial systems, in which the normal channels of money and credit creation were disrupted.

By the late 1940s, basic Keynesian theory had fallen out of favor. Among other prominent economists, Paul Samuelson and James Tobin set about making it more robust and incorporating some of the elements of classical economics, introducing what became known as Neo-Keynesian economics. In particular, Neo-Keynesian economics made much use of quantitative time-series analysis, something which by the 1940s had become much easier to perform due to new mathematical techniques and also to the greater availability of robust historical economic data.

Due to an inability to properly predict or model the stagflationary 1970s, and increasingly challenged by Rational Expectations Theory (RET), Monetarism and the economists of the so-called "Chicago School", including Milton Friedman, Neo-Keynesianism eventually incorporated some of the key tenets of RET and Monetarism. This synthesis led to the creation of New Keynesian Economics.

In general, New Keynesian economists believe that while government deficit spending is an essential policy tool at certain times, monetary policy is generally more appropriate for managing "normal" business cycles in which there is little credit impairment evident. Even in the case of severe credit impairment, central banks can do much in terms of unconventional monetary policy to help moderate downturns and mitigate financial crises. Ideally, monetary and fiscal policies should be coordinated to achieve the desired macroeconomic results.

This book is highly critical of Neo- or New Keynesian Economics, and therefore of the current economic mainstream, for a variety of reasons that will become evident over the course of the text. But it is intellectually dishonest and simply unfair to attack an idea without first presenting it, as I have done here.

CHAPTER 3

Of Bubbles and Bailouts

Surely difficult challenges lie ahead for the Fed, some undoubtedly of our own making.
— Fed Chairman Alan Greenspan, August 27, 2005

Things were looking rather grim for the U.S. economy in mid-1987, soon after Paul Volcker left his job at the helm of the Federal Reserve. The dollar was falling, fast. Inflation and inflation expectations were rising. It was clear that the Fed was going to need to start raising interest rates soon, perhaps sharply. Having successfully broken the back of inflation and supported the dollar in the early 1980s with explicit monetary targeting, double-digit interest rates, and the most severe post–World War II recession to date, financial markets were naturally increasingly fearful that the Fed might follow a similar if less severe script again. While the exact trigger will perhaps never be known, this was the fundamental economic backdrop that led to the great stock market crash of October 19, 1987, when the Dow Jones Industrial Average declined by 23 percent (Figure 3.1).[1]

[1]Several triggers for Black Monday have been proposed in a number of papers. One relatively recent study was prepared by Federal Reserve staff and listed rising global interest rates, a weaker dollar, and a rising U.S. trade deficit as potential fundamental, macroeconomic causes and a proposed corporate tax change, listed options expiry, and large redemptions from a prominent mutual fund group as potential immediate triggers. See Mark Carlson, *A Brief History of the 1987 Stock Market Crash with a Discussion of the Federal Reserve Response*, Federal Reserve Board of Governors Finance and Economic Discussion Series, 2006, www.federalreserve.gov/pubs/feds/2007/200713/200713pap.pdf.

Figure 3.1   The Falling Dollar Was a Key Part of the Fundamental Background of the 1987 Crash (Federal Reserve Trade Weighted Dollar Index)
Source: Federal Reserve.

Alan Greenspan, a veteran of U.S. economic policy-making circles but a neophyte at the Fed, sensed correctly that an emergency easing of interest rates and other liquidity-enhancing measures would help to restore confidence in the equity market, financial system, and economy generally and prevent a possible recession. Sure enough, equity markets bounced sharply in the following days and continued to climb steadily in the following months, recovering all losses with what seemed little effort.

This episode was most certainly a baptism by fire for Greenspan and one that, no doubt, taught him at least one important lesson: If done quickly and communicated properly to the financial markets, emergency Fed policy actions can provide swift and dramatic support for asset prices. But at what cost?

Although Greenspan might consider this his first major crisis-management success, was the Fed's policy reaction to the 1987 crash proportionate or even appropriate? Was it an equal but opposite reaction that merely temporarily stabilized financial markets or did it, in fact, implicitly expand the Fed's regulatory role to managing equity prices? Indeed, one could argue that this was merely the first of a series of progressively larger, so called Greenspan "puts" that the Fed would provide to the financial markets during the 18 years that the "Maestro" was in charge of monetary policy and, let's not forget, bank regulation.

Having received a shot in the arm from the abrupt easing of monetary conditions in late 1987, as well as the lagged effects of a much weaker dollar, the U.S. Consumer Price Index rose more than 5 percent year over year in early 1989, and the Fed raised rates in response, eventually tipping the economy into a recession. One aspect of the 1990–1993 recession that received much comment and analysis was the double dip. Whereas the initial phase of the recession looked like a fairly typical business investment and inventory cycle, the second phase was characterized by a general credit crunch that constrained growth in most areas of the economy. What was the cause of this credit crunch? Why, the long-forgotten savings and loan crisis, of course.

The Forgotten U.S. Housing Bubble

The American dream of home ownership, although associated with the U.S. economy's capitalist tradition, is apparently something that cannot be achieved without ever-growing government regulation and subsidies. Politicians just love finding ways to assist their constituents with home purchases. In some cases, there is so much government help available that home owners end up owning homes they can't afford. In the 1980s, Congress decided that, to make housing more affordable, it would ease certain regulations previously restricting the lending activities of savings and loans (S&Ls). Credit would thereby become more widely available to a range of borrowers who previously might not have qualified. Importantly, this included risky commercial lending.[2]

Seeking higher returns, some S&Ls broadened their lending activities, expanded their balance sheets, and focused more and more on the riskiest, most lucrative opportunities. As S&Ls were financed primarily by deposits, they needed to offer more attractive deposit rates to expand. But because all deposits were insured in equal measure by the Federal Savings and Loan Insurance Corporation (FSLIC, the S&L equivalent of the Federal Deposit Insurance Corporation), depositors would shop around, seeking out the best

[2]A reasonably complete timeline of the key events leading up to the S&L crisis is provided by the FDIC at www.fdic.gov/bank/historical/s&l/.

rates. Deposits therefore flowed from the more conservative to the riskiest institutions offering the highest rates on deposits—fully insured, of course. Some of the most aggressive S&Ls went on a shopping spree, snapping up their more conservative counterparts and deploying their newly acquired deposits into the latest, greatest, high-risk, high-return ventures.

The results were predictable. By the late 1980s, a sizeable portion of the S&L industry was insolvent. The recession of 1990–1991 made a bad situation worse. The FSLIC funds were rapidly depleted. But a federal guarantee is supposed to be just that, a guarantee, so Congress put together a bailout package for the industry. A new federal agency, the Resolution Trust Corporation (RTC), issued bonds fully backed by the U.S. Treasury and used the proceeds to make insolvent S&L depositors whole.

All of this took time, however, and as the bad assets of the S&Ls were worked off, the economy entered part two of the double dip, and the credit crunch intensified. The Fed, however, knew what to do. By taking the Fed funds rate all the way down to 3 percent, real interest rates were effectively zero for the first time since the 1970s (Figure 3.2). The Fed then held them there for nearly two years, finally raising them in early 1994, when it was absolutely clear that the economy was recovering strongly and the credit crunch was over.

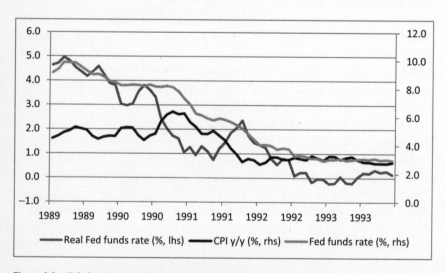

Figure 3.2   U.S. Real Interest Rates Were Effectively Zero in 1992–1993

Source: Federal Reserve.

Fast-forward a decade. We all know that the origins of the most recent boom and bust in U.S. housing and credit can generally be traced back to the highly accommodative Fed policy implemented in the wake of the dot-com bust in 2001–2003. By late 2003, there was clear evidence that the U.S. housing market was surging, and homeowners were extracting record amounts of equity from their homes, thereby stimulating the broader economy. However, amid relatively low consumer price inflation, the Fed determined—incorrectly, we now know—that interest rates should rise only slowly, notwithstanding the surge in asset prices.

With the Fed moving slowly and predictably, risk premia for essentially all assets plummeted. In a Fed policy speech in the mid-2000s, Greenspan referred to the "conundrum" of low term premia for U.S. Treasury bonds. But low credit spreads for corporate bonds and low implied volatilities for nearly all assets were clear evidence of inappropriately loose Fed policy all the way into early 2007.

By the time the subprime mortgage crisis hit in mid-2007, the economic damage had been done. There had been vast overconsumption at home and overinvestment around the world, resulting collectively in perhaps the most monumental misallocation of resources, outside of wartime, in world history. There was no avoiding the subsequent, inevitable crash; the new challenge quickly became how to prevent a complete collapse of the financial system. At this point, the crisis acquired an overt political dimension as U.S. and some other countries' taxpayers were asked, in various direct and indirect ways, to bail out those institutions at risk of insolvency and default.

In retrospect, the entire U.S. S&L debacle, from its origins in regulatory changes and government guarantees, through the risky lending boom, bust, credit crunch, and fiscal and monetary bailout can be seen as a precursor to the far larger global credit bubble and bust of 2003 to the present (Figure 3.3): Just replace the S&Ls with Fannie and Freddie and the international "shadow banking system." But there is no need to change the massive moral hazard perpetrated by incompetent government regulators, including, of course, the Fed, and the reckless and greedy financial firms that played essentially the same role in both episodes.

Those at all surprised by current efforts by the Fed and other regulatory bodies to expand their power over the financial system

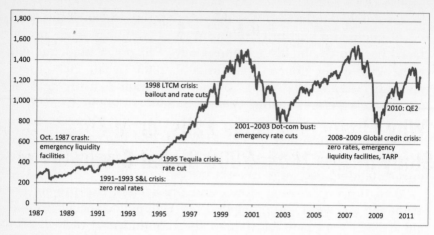

Figure 3.3   See the Pattern? For Every Crisis There Is a Bailout: S&P 500 Index, 1987–Present
Source: Standard & Poor's.

and the economy in general have not been paying attention to history: For every market action, there is a disproportionate regulatory and monetary policy reaction that increases the moral hazard of the system, laying the foundations for an even greater crisis in future. History may not repeat, but it certainly rhymes, as we explore in some detail in the Chapter 4.

CHAPTER

4

Why Financial Genius Fails, or, a Forensic Study of the 2008–2009 Global Credit Crisis

The U.S. economy is in danger of a recession that will prove unusually severe and long. . . . The great question is what will happen to the variety of financial asset bubbles in the United States when the housing bubble bursts and the economy slumps.

—Kurt Richebaecher, former Chief Economist of Dresdner Bank, 2006

Much excellent analysis has already been written regarding the origins and key events of the 2008–2009 global credit crisis. In this chapter, I am not going to flog a dead horse. I am, however, going to explore some of the subtler ways in which the moral hazard created by U.S. economic policy in the period 1987–2006 contributed to the near-collapse of the financial system in late 2008.

The key lesson is that the U.S. monetary, economic, and financial regulatory regime does not promote stability but, in fact, undermines it. As such, the U.S. financial system is inherently unstable and fundamentally at odds with the current global fiat dollar reserve currency standard, which we elaborate on later.

A Brief History of Failed Financial Genius

The dustbin of financial history is littered with examples of failed genius, in which extraordinarily bright, determined, hugely successful financiers or traders encounter a set of circumstances that take even them by surprise, and, lo and behold, they go suddenly, sometimes spectacularly, bankrupt. Long-Term Capital Management (LTCM), a large hedge fund that employed several Nobel Prize winners yet failed in 1998, threatening the entire U.S. financial system, is a high-profile example, but there are many more. No doubt there were also clever folks involved in running the Knickerbocker Trust (failed 1907), Austrian Kreditanstalt (1931), Continental Illinois National Bank (1984), more than 1,000 U.S. savings and loans (1986–1991), Barings UK (1995), and, of course, Bear Stearns, Lehman Brothers, Merrill Lynch, Washington Mutual, and Wachovia (2008).

No doubt equally clever people were running the myriad hedge funds and funds of funds that have been forced in recent years, for one reason or another, to close their doors. As we know, during the past decade, huge numbers of math, science, and engineering graduates and PhDs from the world's best universities entered the financial industry and went to work building subprime collateralized debt obligations (CDOs), among other toxic securities, that have lost most or, in some cases, all of their value. There was certainly plenty of genius to go around—too much, perhaps.

Perhaps hiring geniuses doesn't guarantee that your firm won't go bankrupt or that it won't threaten the broader financial system. But what if it made it even more likely? What if some of the very geniuses who have been involved with financial failures in the past and are now the authorities on what exactly went wrong and what needs to be done, or avoided, to prevent future crises are, in fact, drawing wrong, potentially dangerous conclusions?

Let's focus this discussion on the observations of a gentleman getting much press of late, Jim Rickards, author of the recently published book *Currency Wars* and former general counsel to LTCM. In a 2010 interview, he explained what he believes are perhaps the key reasons why the financial industry so badly miscalculated the risks it was taking going into the recent crisis:

> As general counsel of LTCM, I negotiated the bailout, which averted an even greater disaster at that point. What strikes me now, looking back, is how nothing was changed; no lessons were applied. Even though the lessons were obvious, in 1998. LTCM

used fatally flawed VAR risk models. LTCM used too much leverage.[1]

These value at risk (VAR) risk models to which Rickards refers are models that assume that financial asset price movements are normally distributed; that is, they follow a bell-shaped curve under which one standard deviation from the mean encompasses roughly two-thirds of all potential outcomes, and by the time you have moved three standard deviations away, you capture some 99 percent of all outcomes. That leaves the 1 percent, which is known in the industry as a once-in-a-century event—so unlikely that, for practical business purposes, there is little if any reason to worry about it.

The importance of the assumption that financial variables are normally distributed should not be underestimated. It is central to essentially all aspects of modern finance, ranging from how assets are to be valued, to how much capital traders, funds, or banks should hold against leveraged positions. As an example, the original Black-Scholes option pricing model, developed in the 1970s and for which the Nobel Prize in Economics was awarded in 1997, assumes a normal distribution. Although subsequently modified in various ways, option pricing models in use today still explicitly assume the normality—bell-curve distribution—of returns.

Rickards is quite right that VAR is a fatally flawed concept. There is overwhelming evidence that financial price returns are not normally distributed but rather follow what is known in physics as a power curve distribution. Rickards describes this as:

> . . . a different kind of degree distribution. Any degree distribution is simply a plotting of the frequency of an event relative to the severity of the event. . . . A power curve, one of the most common degree distributions in nature, which accurately describes many phenomena, has fewer low impact events than the bell curve but has far more high impact events. . . .
>
> A power curve says that events of any size can happen and that extreme events happen more frequently than the bell curve

[1]This quote, and all subsequent quotes from Rickards in this chapter, are taken from a fascinating interview by Kathryn Welling in *Welling@Weeden* 12, no. 4 (2010). We take this opportunity to thank *Welling@Weeden* for permission to use these quotes.

suggests. This corresponds to the market behavior we have seen in such extreme events as the crash of 1987, LTCM's collapse, the dot.com bubble's bursting in 2000, the housing collapse in 2007—you get the idea. Statistically, these events should happen once every 1,000 years or so in a bell curve distribution—but are expected much more frequently in a power curve distribution. In short, a power curve describes market reality, while a bell curve does not. . . .

Bell curve distributions in this context describe continuous phenomena and power laws describe discontinuous but regular phenomena.

Now we notice here two things: First, Rickards is a seriously intelligent fellow with significant direct market experience and superior statistical knowledge. Second, and far subtler but hugely important, we see that the financial industry as a whole has chosen to embrace VAR models, notwithstanding overwhelming evidence that they dramatically underestimate risk. If the financial world is populated by geniuses, what possible explanation could there be for that? Well, he has an explanation:

[T]he history of science is filled with false paradigms that gained followers to the detriment of better science. People really did believe the sun revolved around the earth for 2,000 years and mathematicians had the equations to prove it. . . . In effect, once an intellectual concept attracts a critical mass of supporters, it becomes entrenched. . . .

I don't know whether it was denial or inertia or because people got so wedded to the elegance of the mathematics they'd done that they hated to leave all that work behind. . . . In other words, Wall Street decided that the wrong map is better than no map at all—as long as the maths are elegant. And that led to calling extreme events a sort of special case, a "fat tail," which just meant they were happening more frequently than a bell curve would indicate.

Perhaps that's it. But no, that's not all. Rickards goes one step further, which, given the huge rise in proprietary trading activities in recent decades, rings true:

[A]nother reason the Street was loath to throw out the whole notion of normally distributed risk, and tried to salvage it instead by putting a fat tail on it, is that the alternative, a power curve, just didn't look that palatable to most practitioners and so comparatively little work has been done in applying power curves to financial markets. . . .

The thing is, power curves don't have a lot of predictive value. Since most financial researchers approach the field precisely to gain a trading edge, once they discover power curves aren't much use there, they move on. . . .

Good insight. Probably spot on. The consequences, as we know, have been devastating. Rickards uses the severity yet unpredictability of earthquakes as an excellent analogy for financial crises and for what he believes should be done to avoid them in future:

We know that 8.0 earthquakes are possible and we build cities accordingly, even if we cannot know when the big one will strike. Likewise, we can use power curve analysis to make our financial system more robust even if we cannot predict financial earthquakes. And one of its lessons is that as you increase the scale of the system, the risk of a mega-earthquake goes up exponentially. . . .

Unfortunately, this is not something that Wall Street or its various regulators currently comprehend. After all, the institutions that were too big to fail back in 2008 are even larger now, posing a greater systemic threat.

But I'm not so easily convinced of Wall Street's ignorance in this matter. I will explain why in a moment. First, allow Rickards to continue with his explanation:

I've always thought the problem was that, although Wall Street was very active in hiring a lot of PhDs—astrophysicists, applied mathematicians and others with very good quantitative theoretical skills, it didn't let them use their heads. What happened was that their Wall Street managers said, "Look, here's how the financial world works and we want you to model it and code it and develop it and write these equations and programs." And so they did. . . . [I]nstead of telling them what to do, they should have listened.

Now, why is that, do you think? As mentioned earlier, I have an idea. Those Wall Street managers telling their quants what techniques to use were clever enough to understand that, were they to employ models based on power curve distributions, it would not make proprietary trading any more profitable, as such models lack predictive power. But it would dramatically increase their cost of capital, as their capital bases would need to be large enough to ensure against power-curve-implied earthquakes. Capital would need to increase, and balance sheet leverage decrease exponentially, alongside any growth in proprietary trading operations. How convenient and coincidental that Wall Street executives collectively created a VAR-based risk management culture at every single major trading firm, without exception, notwithstanding the overwhelming historical evidence that VAR is fatally flawed!

Perhaps Rickards is just being polite. I have no such compunctions when it comes to entertaining ideas of possible conflicts of interest between Wall Street executives and their firms' shareholders. The evidence may be circumstantial, but in my opinion it is clear. It was never in Wall Street's interest to seriously consider replacing VAR-based with power-curve-based risk management because it would have raised the cost of capital, thereby curtailing profits, salaries, and bonuses.

But wait a minute: Am I implying that Wall Street executives were willing to risk the bankruptcy of their own firms and even the collapse of the entire financial system by deliberately employing far too much leverage? Yes, I am. As a managing director at multiple major global financial institutions in the period 2000–2008, I had ample opportunity to observe the prevailing attitudes toward risk at the highest levels, and also how key decisions were made. There was a consistent, clear bias in favor of risk-taking, with risk-management playing only a supporting, enabling role. Those taking the greatest risks generally received the greatest rewards, including, importantly, rapid promotion. The executive committees of the major firms were thus comprised overwhelmingly of those most successful at pushing risk-taking to its practical limit, which included placating (or, in some instances, bullying) those in risk-management.

Remember, these Wall Street executives are smart guys. Perhaps as smart as Newton. Perhaps as smart as Rickards. Perhaps smarter still: So smart that they took a good look back at post–World War II financial market history and saw that *in every single instance in which the threat of systemic failure arose, policymakers intervened with progressively greater assistance.* And in every instance, the policy reaction has proven, in hindsight, to be disproportionate to the crisis, and the moral hazard implicit in the system has grown. Indeed, it could be argued that the regulators have made the financial world safe for fundamentally flawed, VAR-based risk models. If the power curve distribution does indeed obtain, and the 2008–2009 crisis provides crystal clear evidence that it does, then given that the too-big-to-fail firms are now even larger than they were prior to the Lehman Brothers bailout, an even larger financial crisis, with an even larger bailout price tag, lurks in the not-so-distant future.

(At the time of writing, a crisis an order of magnitude greater than that sparked by the Lehman Brothers failure appears to be brewing in the euro-area banking system, which has a huge net exposure to the heavily overindebted nations of Greece, Ireland, Portugal, Spain, and even Italy, which has the third-largest government debt in the entire world. The ECB has responded by purchasing incremental portions of these countries' debts and also by providing unprecedented three-year financing to euro-area banks. While such actions do buy time, they don't in any way address the underlying causes of the crisis, that is, the excessive debt and leverage in the system.)

A Regulatory Silver Bullet?

Regardless of whether Rickards believes, as I do, that Wall Street executives deliberately chose to ignore the implications of the power curve distribution or were simply blissfully unaware, he has specific recommendations for how to avoid another major financial crisis:

> [O]nce we understand the structure and vulnerability of the financial system in this way, some solutions and policy recommendations become obvious. . . .
>
> They fall into three categories: limiting scale, controlling cascades and securing informational advantage. . . .
>
> I certainly would favor the Volcker Rule and I would favor bringing back something like Glass-Steagall. And I'd favor imposing stricter capital ratios on banks and brokers.

What these recommendations collectively would do is give substantially greater power to regulators to determine how Wall Street is run. But stop right there. Is this realistic? Who, exactly, is going to determine how to limit scale? How can we have any confidence that such decisions will not be highly politicized? By controlling cascades, are regulators not providing an implicit subsidy for excessive risk taking? Rickards might counter that his proposed stricter capital ratios would limit such risk taking, but once again, can we be at all confident that such capital ratios will be set in a sensible, objective, nonpoliticized way, given the history of chronic failures on the part of regulators to effectively carry out their mandates? (The most recent such example of regulatory failure appears to be the MF Global bankruptcy, where client funds, thought to be segregated, were in fact used as collateral for proprietary positions. If true, this demonstrates at a minimum persistent regulatory incompetence or, alternatively, regulatory complicity in fraudulent practices at the highest levels of the U.S. financial system.)

My concern with a purely regulatory-based solution to serial financial crises come down to the following: Is Rickards really prepared to place his faith in the regulators who enabled the S&Ls to embark on their fateful 1980s lending binge, who failed to see the dot-com bubble but then wasted no time slashing rates when the market crashed, who denied that there was a housing bubble even as they were claiming that the nascent subprime crisis was contained, who were supposedly overseeing Fannie and Freddie in the years prior to bailing them out completely, who repeatedly missed (or chose not to hear) the warnings about Bernie Madoff, who glossed over Lehman 105 repo transactions, and who bailed out AIG Credit Default Swaps (CDS) at par even though such contracts were trading at a huge discount in the market?

To be fair, Rickards is in good company. There are numerous policy makers and financial commentators who appear not to have learned the lesson that the U.S. financial regulatory regime not only repeatedly fails but fails so completely, consistently, and predictably that Wall Street has made a highly profitable business out of being bailed out. As Sir Isaac Newton might ask, have these folks fumbling about for a regulatory-based solution to Wall Street excess thought to apply the scientific method properly, isolating key assumptions and controlling for all factors? If they did, they might see the disturbingly consistent pattern right before their eyes and draw the obvious conclusion.

I agree wholeheartedly with Rickards that VAR is a flawed concept and that a power curve approach to risk management would be a welcome step in the right direction. But with all due respect, I am horrified at the prospect that the dysfunctional U.S. financial regulatory system would be tasked with such an important initiative.

If more such "misregulation" is not the answer, then what is? My proposed solution is as simple as it gets: Throw Wall Street to the wolves. Congress should pass a law making it illegal for the government or any agency thereof, including the Federal Reserve, to provide any form of direct financial assistance whatsoever, under any circumstances, to the nondepositor (e.g., wholesale, interbank) sources of funding for the financial system.

How would financial markets respond? Presumably, absent any explicit or implied guarantees, the share prices of weak financial firms would decline, perhaps to levels implying a high risk of insolvency. The weakest institutions would probably also find that their bonds were trading at a large discount and would find it difficult, if not impossible, to refinance at attractive rates. They would be forced to shrink their balance sheets, if not immediately, then gradually over time. Larger (uninsured) depositors would begin to withdraw funds from those institutions deemed at growing risk of failure and place them in stronger institutions. They would also most probably spread deposits around, seeking greater diversification of risk. In general, capital would flow from weak to strong financial institutions, exactly what is needed to avoid a repeat of 2008.[2]

Shareholders, now aware that assistance would not be forthcoming in a crisis, would demand that financial executives not only increase their respective firms' capital cushions but also devote more resources to and provide greater transparency of risk management.

[2]There are those who would argue that government-funded deposit insurance itself is a form of moral hazard. Rather than enter into such a discussion, I find it simpler to emphasize that were financial shareholders and bond holders to act as if there was no implied bailout for financial firms, they would demand more sensible risk management and higher capital ratios, quite possibly along the lines of what Rickards recommends. Doing away with the FDIC is probably not necessary in this regard.

For institutions taking material proprietary risk in trading or investment banking, a general move back to a partnership model, in which executive wealth is tied to the stability and longer-term survival of the firm and in which conflicts of interest with shareholders and bond holders are minimized, would probably take place. Specifically, shareholders would probably demand that risk management replace flawed VAR-based methodologies with those based on a power curve distribution. What Rickards thinks should be done by chronically incompetent regulators would almost certainly be done in short order by increasingly competent, if imperfect, financial executives, in response to shareholder and bondholder pressure.

Mistakes would still be made. Geniuses aren't perfect. But absent a homogeneous VAR-based risk-management culture, the risk of systemic failure would be all but eliminated. If any one firm grew to the point of posing a systemic risk, the cost of capital for the entire system would rise accordingly, constraining growth and reallocating resources to less risky nonfinancial business sectors.

I believe I know why financial genius fails. The answer is surprisingly simple, really: because failure pays so much better than success. Only when action is taken to ensure that success pays better than failure will financial crises threatening the health of the entire economy become a thing of the past.

Aftermath

Regardless of whether Wall Street firms were aware of the risks they were running or whether policy makers realized that, through the decades, the degree of moral hazard had grown to system-destabilizing proportions is ultimately moot. What matters now is that the crisis has left in its wake a massive mismatch in domestic U.S. and global monetary policy preferences and objectives. This represents a highly unstable equilibrium, which makes the situation in 1971—the year President Nixon suspended gold convertibility—look rather tame by comparison. Therefore, we now turn to a discussion of equilibrium dynamics.

CHAPTER 5

An Unstable Equilibrium

A Nash equilibrium is defined as a strategy combination with the property that every player's strategy is a best reply to the other players' strategies. This of course is true also for Nash equilibria in mixed strategies. But in the latter case, besides his mixed equilibrium strategy, each player will also have infinitely many alternative strategies that are his best replies to the other players' strategies. This will make such equilibria potentially unstable.

— Economist John Harsanyi at the Nobel Prize Seminar
in honor of Mathematician and Economist John Nash, 1994

While as a separate subdiscipline within the economics profession, game theory is relatively new, some of the basic tenets have been around for as long as society itself. At its core, game theory is nothing more than the study of how individuals act in social situations in which there is some degree of competition. *Bargaining* and *haggling* are terms that come to mind. But what sets game theory apart is that it attempts to calculate precisely what the outcome of a given bargaining or haggling session is likely to be.

To do so, game theorists need to make certain assumptions, for example:

- What are the true interests of the players?
- What are their alternatives?

- How might the interests and alternatives of one player be taken into account by the other players?

It is this last question that is at the heart of John Nash's concept of an equilibrium that can be applied to a game with a potentially infinite number of participants. A system (game) can be said to be in equilibrium when no player has a better alternative to their existing behavior (strategy), given the interests and alternatives of the other players.

By way of an example, in a scene from the 2002 film *A Beautiful Mind*, the young John Nash is at a bar with several fellow male PhD students, enjoying a few beers, when in walks a stunning, beautiful, young blond lady, as well as a few of her rather less stunning (if hardly unattractive) brunette girlfriends. At once, he and each of his buddies notice, heads turning in unison toward the stunning young lady, then back to each other. The unasked question among the group is "Who is going to be first to approach her?"

As they all stand up and begin moving toward the stunning blond, young Nash realizes there is a potential problem with what he and his friends are about to do: If all of them try simultaneously to engage the stunner in conversation, thereby essentially ignoring her friends, then it is highly unlikely that she is going to want to remain so engaged for long, regardless of how interesting she might find it personally, as she will be in the uncomfortable position of having the attention of several men at once while her friends have none. The obvious risk is that she and her friends are collectively put off to the point of avoiding the entire group of young men or summarily departing the bar entirely. As such, in the game of determining which of Nash and his friends should first engage the blond in conversation, the solution is . . .

. . . wait for it . . .

None of them!

Why is that? Consider: As it would turn the woman off were all the young men to approach her simultaneously—and as would almost certainly happen in the event that any one of them made a move in that direction—the best solution is for the men to approach her friends instead. This may seem a suboptimal outcome from the isolated perspective of any one of the young men, in that not one of them will have the opportunity of chatting up the stunner, at least not at first. At a minimum, however, they will be chatting up her friends, something they would all agree is a far better alternative to just sitting at their own table and chatting with each other, as on any other normal evening. The strategy that is the best reply to the other players' strategies provides the Nash equilibrium, in this case, the strategy of approaching the stunner's friends and ignoring the stunner herself entirely.

With that example in mind, we can now apply the concept of a Nash equilibrium to the current set of global monetary arrangements —in particular, the central legacy of Bretton Woods, the fiat dollar reserve standard—and consider how recent U.S. and global economic and financial developments have destabilized it. Let us first turn, however, to the pertinent historical example of the rise of the dollar—backed by gold—as a challenger to the pound sterling's nearly exclusive reserve status at the start of the twentieth century.

How World War I Destabilized the Century-Old Sterling Reserve Standard

Although previously linked to gold, the dollar has been the dominant global reserve currency since the 1920s, when it assumed this role from the pound sterling. Already by the end of the nineteenth century, the U.S. economy had surpassed that of the United Kingdom in both industrial power and agricultural output. To be fair, the British Empire in its entirety was certainly larger; however, the cost of maintaining it was vast and growing, amid regional instability and growing military commitments.

The pound sterling assumed global reserve status following the hard-won victory over Napoleonic France in the early nineteenth century. For decades, it had been rather touch-and-go as to whether Britain or France would emerge victorious on the continent and, hence, have the upper hand when it came to expanding the colonial empires that both countries had acquired in the course of the prior century. With Napoleon vanquished, Britain had a relatively free hand in much of the world, with the notable exceptions of the Americas and central Asia. It was not for want of trying, however. Britain took on the young United States for a second time in 1812, only to be fought to a stalemate. And Britain had a go at Russia in the Crimea in the mid-1800s, which turned out more of a defeat, as did its occupation of Afghanistan.

By 1907, as a result of a series of crises in which both the British and French began to regard their respective empires as under threat from an increasingly powerful, unified, and assertive Germany, there was a realignment in European geopolitics. Both the British and French allied with Russia to keep Germany contained (or *eingekreist*—encircled—from the German perspective). When Russia and Germany subsequently clashed in August 1914 over how to respond to the assassination of Austrian Archduke (and heir to the throne) Franz Ferdinand, a general European war broke out.

Regardless of who was most responsible for starting it, World War I was hugely expensive and destructive for all European participants and, tragically, killed or severely injured a substantial portion of the young, productive British workforce. By contrast, although the United States entered the war in 1917, it did so from a position of relative strength, with both sides already nearing exhaustion. By late 1918, following the November armistice U.S. troops began heading home. Although Britain won the war, its government finances did not. By the early-1920s, it was increasingly clear that Britain's economy was struggling to grow while shouldering the twin financial burdens of servicing the huge war debt and maintaining the vast overseas empire.

Having abandoned the gold standard and inflated the currency to help finance the war, Britain did attempt to return to gold in 1925 (although this was poorly executed, as it happens, as we discuss at some length later). Yet the writing was on the wall. Also on the gold standard, yet now with a much larger economy and far sounder government finances behind it, the U.S. dollar was used increasingly in international transactions and as a reserve currency for the global banking system. When in 1931 the British retreated from their return to gold and devalued the pound sterling versus the dollar by some 25%, it was an acknowledgment of what had been occurring beneath the surface of the global economy for years. A new monetary equilibrium had been found with the dollar, not the pound sterling, at the center.

Let's return to Nash and consider how World War I changed the environment in which the game of global monetary relations was being played. One player, Britain, found its economic position severely weakened. Another, the United States, continued to grow rapidly. Not only was the U.S. population growing, so was per capita income. As for other countries, most of them now found they were trading relatively more with the larger and more rapidly growing United States and relatively less with the smaller and stagnating Britain and its empire. See Table 5.1.

Table 5.1   Real GDP per Capita Ratios for Selected Country Pairs

	U.K./United States	U.K./Germany	U.K./France
1870	130.5	173.5	170
1913	92.8	134.9	141.2
1929	79.8	135.8	116.8

Source: Angus Maddison historical database.

It was only natural that more and more trade was not only trans-acted in dollars but also invoiced and accounted for in dollars. Moreover, with a larger, healthier economy standing behind it, the dollar was now also regarded as a more reliable store of value, less likely to be suddenly devalued (as sterling was in 1914 and would again be in 1931). As such, for managing risk, the dollar was increasingly seen as the natural reference point and reserve to hold against potential loss, the preferred reserve currency.

The dollar reserve standard thus became the new global monetary equilibrium, although, of course, the dollar was backed by gold, at a rate of $20.67 per ounce. As the United States became increasingly prosperous in the 1920s—the Roaring 20s—it began to import relatively more and export relatively less to the rest of the world, and the gold reserve began to flow out. In 1926, the United States held fully 45 percent of the entire world's monetary gold supply (excluding Russia). Yet by the early 1930s, this share fell to under 35 percent.

Following World War II, one consequence of which was a huge accumulation of gold by the United States, the share increased briefly to over 60 percent.[1] Yet once again, as the United States began to import and consume more and export relatively less, the share declined steadily thereafter, sinking below 50 percent by the late 1950s. By the mid-1960s, U.S. gold holdings were less than its foreign liabilities. It was precisely this development that so worried the French and other Europeans and led Jacques Rueff, among

[1]While the United States had already accumulated large official gold holdings following FDRs confiscation of private gold in 1934, WWII provided a historic opportunity to acquire gold from abroad amidst the extra-legal chaos of wartime. While the exact amount will perhaps never be known, and has been the topic of innumerable conspiracy theories, it is generally assumed that some portion of the German and Japanese gold hoards were discovered by U.S. forces during or following the war.

other economists, to predict the imminent demise of the Bretton Woods system.[2]

How the 2008–2009 Global Credit Crisis Destabilized Bretton Woods II, or the Fiat-Dollar Reserve Standard

While World War I and the financial crisis of 2008–2009 are hard to compare in many respects, such as the devastation they wrought or their political consequences, they have certain things in common. Both had a huge impact on the health of economies, including that of the country providing the global reserve currency. Both led to economic policy decisions at the national level that were clearly not in the interest of other nations. As such, both destabilized the Nash equilibrium required to maintain a global reserve currency standard.

It is not yet generally appreciated however, the extent to which the 2008–2009 financial crisis and global economic policy responses to it have already fatally undermined the fiat-dollar standard equilibrium. This is due primarily to a misconception within the economics profession that for most, if not all, of the key players involved, the costs of moving away from the fiat-dollar standard still far exceed the benefits.

This view has been the conventional wisdom for some years. In late 2003, three prominent economists, David Folkerts-Landau, Michael Dooley, and Peter Garber, published a paper making the case that the so-called Bretton Woods II arrangement of fixed or generally managed emerging market exchange rates vis-à-vis the dollar—a system that had been more or less in place following the various Asian currency crises of 1997–1998—was a stable equilibrium for a variety of reasons. The most important reason given was that the emerging markets were undergoing a long-term structural investment boom that could be properly financed only through export-led growth, much as had been the case under the original Bretton Woods arrangements in the 1950s and 1960s, when Western Europe and Japan exported their way to renewed postwar prosperity. As such, notwithstanding a declining share of global economic output and rising fiscal and current account deficits, the fiat-dollar

---

[2]For the historical data cited here, see Henry Hazlitt, *What You Should Know about Inflation* (Princeton, NJ: D. Van Nostrand, 1964).

was likely to remain the world's preeminent reserve currency for the foreseeable future, indeed, for decades to come.

Here is the abstract to the paper on the NBER website, which originally appeared in the *International Journal of Finance and Economics*:

The economic emergence of a fixed exchange rate periphery in Asia has reestablished the United States as the center country in the Bretton Woods international monetary system. We argue that the normal evolution of the international monetary system involves the emergence of a periphery for which the development strategy is export-led growth supported by undervalued exchange rates, capital controls and official capital outflows in the form of accumulation of reserve asset claims on the center country. The success of this strategy in fostering economic growth allows the periphery to graduate to the center. Financial liberalization, in turn, requires floating exchange rates among the center countries. But there is a line of countries waiting to follow the Europe of the 1950s/60s and Asia today sufficient to keep the system intact for the foreseeable future.[3]

I was not alone at the time in being somewhat skeptical that this was the case, in particular because as a result of maintaining fixed or managed exchange rates with the United States, not only were the emerging markets growing much faster than the United States but also they were accumulating vast dollar reserves that were then reinvested in U.S. assets, thereby pushing down dollar interest rates and pushing up asset valuations, including, of course, house prices, to levels inconsistent with the potential growth rate of the U.S. economy. But with consumer price inflation low as a result of cheap manufactured goods from abroad and low rents at home—the flip side of the increasing rate of home ownership, courtesy of low interest rates—the U.S. Federal Reserve saw no need to raise rates in response to the domestic credit, housing, and consumption boom, which ultimately originated from the Bretton-Woods II regime. (See Figures 5.1 and 5.2. For Figure 5.1 debt equals total U.S. economy debt, public and private.)

---

[3]The paper can be accessed at www.nber.org/papers/w9971.pdf.

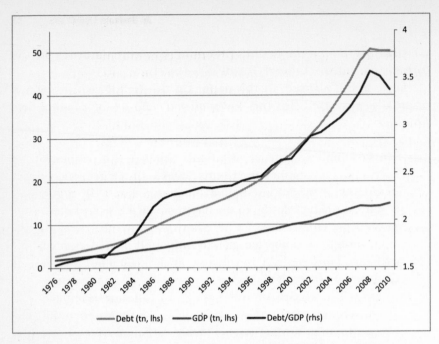

Figure 5.1   The U.S. Fed Stood by, amid Low CPI, Facilitating the Growth of a Colossal Debt Bubble . . .

Source: Federal Reserve.

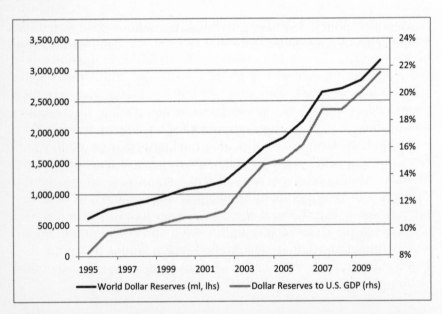

Figure 5.2   . . . Which, As Could Be Seen at the Time, the Debt Bubble Was Being Financed by Foreign Countries Accumulating Dollar Reserves

Source: IMF.

It is now generally accepted by the economic mainstream that the Fed's decision to hold interest rates low for a sustainable period in 2003–2005 was the key contributing cause of the growth of the U.S. housing bubble that burst in 2007, thereby triggering the subsequent global financial crisis. Yet as the bubble was inflating, Fed officials repeatedly claimed that not only was the rise in house prices not a bubble but also that low interest rates had little if anything to do with it. In 2005, Ben Bernanke, who had only recently assumed the Fed chairmanship, claimed that low U.S. borrowing costs were the result of a "global savings glut," in particular in rapidly growing Asian countries, rather than a function of Fed monetary policy.[4] But the global savings glut and Fed policy should never have been separated in this way. The latter directly enabled the former.

By focusing as it did, and for that matter still does, on consumer price inflation only, rather than money and credit growth generally, the Fed completely missed the connection between U.S. interest rates, global savings, investment, and asset prices. It therefore failed to see that its policies were the ultimate cause of the housing bubble and that the "global savings glut" was just one link in a long money-and-credit chain that had become unanchored by misguided or even reckless Fed policy. The late great Austrian school economist Kurt Richebächer recognized clearly that this was the case. As he wrote in April 2005:

In earlier studies published by the International Monetary Fund about asset bubbles in general, and Japan's bubble economy in particular, the authors repeatedly asked why policymakers failed to recognize the rising prices in the asset markets as asset inflation. Their general answer was that the absence of conventional inflation in consumer and producer prices confused most people, traditionally accustomed to taking rises in the CPI as the decisive token for inflation.

It seems to us that today this very same confusion is blinding policymakers and citizens in the United States and other bubble

---

[4]The text of this speech can be found at www.federalreserve.gov/boarddocs/speeches/2005/200503102/.

economies, like England and Australia, to the unmistakable circumstance of existing rampant housing bubbles in their countries.

Thinking about inflation, it is necessary to separate its cause and its effects or symptoms. There is always one and the same cause, and that is credit creation in excess of current saving leading to demand growth in excess of output. But this common cause may produce an extremely different pattern of effects in the economy and its financial system. This pattern of effects is entirely contingent upon the use of the credit excess—whether it primarily finances consumption, investment, imports or asset purchases.

A credit expansion in the United States of close to $10 trillion—in relation to nominal GDP growth of barely $2 trillion over the last four years since 2000—definitely represents more than the usual dose of inflationary credit excess. This is really hyperinflation in terms of credit creation.

In other words, there is tremendous inflationary pressure at work, but it has impacted the economy and the price system very unevenly. The credit deluge has three obvious main outlets: imports, housing and the carry trade in bonds. On the other hand, the absence of strong consumer price inflation is taken as evidence that inflationary pressures are generally absent. Everybody feels comfortable with this (mis) judgment.[5]

The mistake made by Folkerts-Landau, Dooley, and Garber was that they failed to see back in 2003 that the Fed's easy money policy was fueling rampant money and credit growth that, in time, would lead to a colossal global credit crisis. To be fair, the entire economic mainstream missed it, too. But this just begs the question of why. The best explanation is that the modern economics profession focuses primarily on consumer price inflation as a potential source of economic instability, rather than money and credit growth generally. Austrian school economists, such as Richebächer, know better. He was hardly the only Austrian economist to predict the crisis.

[5] See www.gold-eagle.com/gold_digest_05/richebacher042305.html.

A Brief Introduction to the Austrian Economic School

Although long outside the economic mainstream, the Austrian Economic School predates the Keynesian, Monetarist (or Chicago), and Neo-Keynesian schools of thought by many decades. The reason it is called the Austrian School is because several of its most prominent members were Austrian, including Carl Menger, Eugen von Boehm-Bauwerk, Ludwig von Mises, Friedrich Hayek, and Josef Schumpeter.[6]

The central tenet of the Austrian school is that as long as private property rights are secure, a voluntary exchange-based pricing mechanism, commonly referred to as a "free market", creates a spontaneous order that most efficiently allocates resources, labor, and capital across a modern economy. Interventions by authorities to manipulate the pricing mechanism invariably lead to suboptimal economic outcomes.

Unlike other economic schools, Austrian economists are generally critical of modern central banking because they believe that by setting interest rates by diktat, rather than leaving them to the market, the monetary authorities distort rational economic calculation for all manner of economic activity, leading to an endless series of booms, malinvestments, and busts. And with each such cycle, as long as the central bank steps in to rescue the financial system, it creates an ever-growing moral hazard problem that eventually results in the financial system sucking the bulk of the productive resources out of the real, nonfinancial economy.

From that point forward, even if a central bank lowers interest rates to essentially zero, enabling rapid money and credit creation, this gets little traction in real economic activity; rather, it just fuels asset bubbles. Eventually, when it becomes clear to economic agents that the economy is unable to service its accumulated debts with its declining productive potential, a final crisis will ensue that destroys the banking system and, unless backed by gold or something else with intrinsic value, the currency as well.

The late Kurt Richebächer, chief economist of Dresdner Bank, applied Austrian economic analysis to the U.S. economy in the 1990s and 2000s and predicted in some detail exactly how the dot-com and housing booms would turn to busts. In retrospect, he has been proven exactly right in his predictions. Yet despite this demonstrable foresight, he and his fellow contemporary Austrian economists remain outside the mainstream, their no-nonsense views on

(Continued)

[6]We are taking a broad view of the Austrian School here. To some extent, Hayek and, to a much greater extent, Schumpeter drifted away from the stricter views held by their predecessors. Modern-day Austrians disagree as to whether either or both of them should be included, in particular, Schumpeter.

economics unwelcome to those who pretend that by some hermetic knowledge hidden deeply within the profession, economists can work magic.

Indeed, perhaps the simplest way to understand what sets the Austrian apart from other economic schools is that it is the one that assumes there is no free lunch. It simply does not believe that it is possible for any form of economic command, regulation, confiscatory taxation, or subsidy to improve on the economic outcomes produced naturally and spontaneously by a free, voluntary-exchange market in goods, services, and even money itself. Indeed, market interventions are inevitably counterproductive.

As an aside, there is also a social element to the Austrian school. As the economy is a creation of society, it should serve social ends, not merely economic ones. The fact that people generally prefer to take voluntary rather than coerced action in all aspects of life, economic and otherwise, is recognized by the Austrian school, and so individual liberty is of paramount importance. Ultimately, free societies and free markets go hand-in-hand; you can't have one without the other, a point to which we return at the end of this book.

Today, primarily in the United States but also in certain other countries with classical liberal economic and political traditions, there is a flourishing, alternative school of moral and political thought known as Austro-Libertarianism that combines the economic precepts of the Austrian school with the social precepts of traditional, Lockean-Jeffersonian liberalism.

Interestingly, none other than a young Alan Greenspan was strongly influenced by an early form of Austro-Libertarianism, which we explore in greater detail later in this book.

The Futility of Inflation Targeting

The bulk of the developed economies' central banks follow some sort of inflation-targeting policy regarding consumer price inflation. The Fed and the European Central Bank (ECB) both have dual mandates, although these are somewhat different. In the Fed's case, the goal is to maintain low and stable inflation while also achieving full employment. In the ECB's case, the goal is also to maintain low consumer price inflation but also to prevent money growth accelerating to levels that would imply potentially destabilizing credit growth.

The Fed's mandate is in effect a Keynesian one, in that it assumes that there is some theoretical trade-off between inflation and employment and that the central bank can manage this trade-off in practice, thereby maintaining economic stability and achieving a healthy, sustainable rate of economic growth. As we have seen, however, the Fed has failed to do so, primarily because of the serial bubbles and busts that it has engendered by failing to maintain stable money and credit growth and encouraging excessive risk taking with repeated bailouts. As such, the Fed's mandate is misspecified: Not only is there no simple trade-off between inflation and unemployment, as demonstrated by the stagflationary 1970s and as seen again today, but by the time excessive money and credit growth show up in the consumer price index (CPI), enormous damage may already have been done to the economy and financial system. The CPI is inflation past. Money supply and credit growth is inflation present. And as we shall see later, fiscal deficits are inflation future.

The ECB's mandate, on the other hand, recognizes that there must be some link between money and credit growth, on the one hand, and price stability on the other. It has no set monetary rule but, rather, uses money and credit growth aggregates as an important guide to policy. Thus the ECB's mandate leans a bit in the direction of the Austrian economic tradition.

As it turns out, in sharp contrast to the Fed, the ECB has generally met its inflation target in the decade for which it has been in existence. On multiple occasions, the ECB has raised interest rates, not because growth was particularly strong nor because consumer price inflation had risen significantly, but rather because money and credit growth were elevated and accelerating, implying a rising risk of economic instability in the future. Yes, the ECB came under much criticism at these times, as money and credit targeting had generally fallen out of favor. But the results speak for themselves. In the years 1999 through 2011, the ECB has done the better job.

Recently, the euro area has been beset by a series of sovereign debt crises that threaten the European monetary union (EMU). However, the ECB is not responsible for the chronic overborrowing of various European governments. These crises are fiscal in origin, rather than monetary. It is true that a number of European banks hold large amounts of sovereign debt that is likely to be restructured in some way and that in some cases the banks lack sufficient capital to take the necessary write-downs and still remain solvent. But here, too, it would be incorrect to blame the ECB, which is not the European banking regulator. Within the EMU, bank regulation remains at the national level.

The relative experience of the Fed and the ECB in recent years demonstrates that central banks' focus on inflation targeting is misplaced. The focus must instead be on money and credit growth. But the problem then becomes, if the Fed, the issuer of the world's de facto reserve currency, is not willing to change its ways and follow a mandate that can provide a sufficient degree of global monetary stability, what is the world to do? Switch to the euro? Unfortunately, the various, escalating euro-area sovereign debt crises obviate that possibility. The yen perhaps? Few would take that possibility seriously, given the chronic quantitative easing and foreign exchange intervention of the Japanese authorities. The Swiss franc? No, the Swiss have recently pegged their currency to the euro, removing its potential to serve as an independent monetary reference point.

What of other candidates? Is there any currency out there that both represents a stable economic area and is also managed in a way that would provide sufficient global monetary stability? While there is no national currency that ticks both of those critical boxes, there has been some discussion about turning to the special drawing rights (SDR) unit of account used by the IMF, which could, in theory at least, provide a global fiat reserve currency alternative to the dollar.

The SDR Nonsolution to Global Monetary Instability

The SDR is a basket of IMF member countries' currencies and is used as a unit of account in the IMF's financing and lending activities. As it stands now, the dollar is the largest part of the SDR basket. However, the basket is reweighted whenever member countries' relative capital contributions to the IMF change. Were the BRICs to contribute substantial capital to the IMF, for example, then their currencies could be a substantial portion of the SDR basket. As such, so the thinking goes, the SDR is well-suited to accommodate the shifting, global economic and monetary power equilibrium and therefore provide a proper global fiat currency to succeed the fiat dollar.

However, to turn the SDR from a mere unit of account into a true global reserve currency would take a series of steps, some of which would be politically difficult due to the degree of cooperation involved. First, the IMF would go from being a supranational bank to supranational central bank, with the authority to print and control the global, SDR-denominated money supply. As was the case with the euro at inception, this would not require that actual printed SDR currency circulates; rather, it could be done by the IMF fixing the exchange rates between all member currencies to the SDR reference basket. Recall that from 1999 to 2002, the euro existed as an electronic currency only, with the printed national legacy currencies providing the circulating medium. But from 1999, the ECB nevertheless controlled the collective money supply and set a single interest rate for the entire euro-area banking system. The same could be the case with the SDR indefinitely. National currencies need never be replaced.

In theory, this solves the dilemma of the current fiat dollar reserve system in that it would no longer be the case that a single national central bank indirectly sets international interest rates and controls the global money supply. Rather than dollar reserves providing the greater portion of the global monetary base, the SDR would do so. The IMF would set interest rates and grow the money supply in a way that would serve the broader interests of all IMF member countries. As the IMF describes the proposal in a recent working paper on the topic:

> A limitation of the SDR . . . is that it is not a currency. Both the SDR and SDR-denominated instruments need to be converted eventually to a national currency for most payments or interventions in foreign exchange markets, which adds to cumbersome use in transactions. . . .
>
> A global currency . . . issued by a global central bank would be designed as a stable store of value that is not tied exclusively to the conditions of any particular economy. As trade and finance continue to grow rapidly and global integration increases, the importance of this broader perspective is expected to continue growing. . . .
>
> If [a global currency] were to circulate as a parallel currency but in a dominant role in place of the U.S. dollar, then as in the [system] described above, current account imbalances that reflect today's situation—namely, surplus countries pegging to [the global currency] with deficit countries floating against it—would adjust more symmetrically, and perhaps more

automatically, than the current [system] since the deficit currencies would be expected to depreciate against [the global
currency]. . . .[7]

While this sounds nice on paper, consider it in practice, with the
experience of the euro area over the past decade as a reference
point. The euro was intended to replace national currencies and to
facilitate balance-of-payments adjustments just as the IMF argues
could be done with the SDR globally. Yet it hasn't worked. One monetary policy has not been suitable for all, notwithstanding a tremendous degree of European economic integration. Yes, the ECB has
arguably done a respectable job at balancing the contrasting economic conditions across the euro area, but it is precisely this operational competence that exposes the systemic flaw for all to see. The
fact is that labor and capital have not been mobile enough in the
euro area, resulting in local asset bubbles and excessive wage growth
in the periphery. Fiscal policy has not been sufficiently uniform. And
as the years have passed, the associated imbalances have grown to the
point that the currency union, as currently structured, cannot long
continue. Either there must be a far greater degree of economic
integration—something you cannot force by policy over any reasonable time horizon—or there must be a fiscal union, with automatic
transfer payments from wealthy regions to poorer ones.

Notwithstanding close political ties across borders, few observers
believe that the euro area could implement the degree of fiscal
integration required to make the currency union sustainable without
subverting democracy to a point that would begin to look autocratic
and arbitrary and, as such, blatantly incompatible with modern
European democratic traditions.

Now extrapolate this to the global level. Labor and capital are
far less mobile around the world than within the euro area. Fiscal
policy is far from uniform. Indeed, there are completely different
economic models followed across the world, even if, in general, there
has been a trend toward greater liberalization of labor and capital
markets in recent decades. Imagine now that a push was made for

[7]"Reserve Accumulation and International Monetary Stability," IMF Policy Paper,
prepared by the Strategy, Policy and Review Department, in collaboration with the
Finance, Legal, Monetary and Capital Markets, Research, and Statistics Departments and consultation with the Area Departments, April 13, 2010.

fiscal union among IMF member countries. It is difficult to believe that democratic countries would choose to move in that direction. As for more autocratic ones, some might and some might not, but few could doubt that such decisions would be driven by raw national interest and not some misplaced hope that what has failed demonstrably at the European level would somehow fare better globally.

The degree of cooperation involved to move the world toward an SDR-based single currency is insurmountable in the current global political, social, and economic context, no matter how much monetary sense it might theoretically make. That said, even on the purely monetary side of the issue, it is highly questionable that even the most qualified central bankers in charge of a hypothetical global central bank could possibly make consistently sensible decisions for how to set global interest rates, grow the money supply, act as a lender of last resort in a crisis, and so on.

Among others, Nobel laureate Robert Mundell is highly critical of the possibility that the SDR could somehow replace the fiat dollar as the new primary global monetary reserve asset. As he said in March 2011:

> Today there is no possibility of the SDR or any variant of it becoming a world currency in the sense of a substitute for the role of the dollar in its heyday.[8]

It is understandable that the IMF is making a push to become the issuer of a global currency and serve as the world's central bank. Bureaucrats are naturally drawn to bureaucratic solutions to real-world problems. But as just demonstrated before, a single global fiat currency, based on the SDR or some other arbitrary unit of account, is nothing more than a bureaucratic pipe dream. It is highly unlikely that a global political consensus could be reached for how to construct, share power, and implement policy through a global central

---

[8]Presentation to the China G-20 Seminar, Nanjing, China, March 31, 2011. Mundell does, however, see it as possible, and desirable, that the United States, euro-area, and China agree to fix their exchange rates, so as to provide a stable, global currency anchor for all others. This, he believes, would be a viable replacement for the fiat dollar. In my opinion, given the demonstrably divergent domestic monetary incentives between the United States, China, and within the euro-area itself, it is unrealistic to believe that the actors involved could achieve the degree of agreement and cooperation required to maintain fixed exchange rates for long.

bank. And if it were, the large cracks in this highly unstable Nash equilibrium would spread rapidly at the first signs of crisis, with one country after another defecting, and the entire thing would collapse, leaving the world no better off than it was under the fiat dollar reserve system, and arguably even worse.

The ever-prescient Jacques Rueff was making precisely these points back in the late 1960s, when the newly created SDR unit of account was already seen as a potential successor to the fiat dollar. In particular, he noted that an SDR reserve system would implicitly reward countries that ran budget and trade deficits and penalize those that did not. This is because SDRs could be created to settle balance-of-payments deficits. Those countries running deficits would be the first to receive the new SDRs. In time, however, these new SDRs, a form of global monetary inflation, would contribute to asset bubbles, resource misallocation and consumer price inflation. As such, countries exercising restraint in domestic fiscal and monetary policy would bear the costs for others' profligacy. He was particularly concerned about what would happen when a crisis arose:

> Any international monetary crisis, any major outflow of capital . . . will provide an opportunity for an inflationary issue of SDRs. This in turn will lead to powerful surges of inflation in creditor countries.[9]

An SDR-based system would thus suffer from an inherent moral-hazard problem encouraging deficit spending and domestic inflation, which would periodically spill over into international monetary crises. Under Bretton-Woods, only the United States enjoyed the "exorbitant privilege" of being able to effectively force creditor countries to finance its trade and budget deficits at low interest rates. Under an SDR-based system, any country running trade and budget deficits would have the privilege.

The idea that China, Japan, Russia, oil exporters, or other creditor countries would go along with such a scheme is absurd. Absent a hegemon to impose it, the idea that agreement could be reached to enact such as arrangement and sustain it thereafter is far-fetched indeed.

[9]Jacques Rueff, *The Monetary Sin of the West* (New York: The Macmillan Company, 1970), 171.

Were Jacques Rueff alive today, he would probably see an SDR-based solution as even more unworkable than in the late 1960s, given the current degree of monetary instability and lack of global competition, both of which are an order of magnitude greater. Fortunately, no fiat currency, national or global, is required to serve as the primary global reserve. History presents the world with an existing, tried, and tested alternative: gold.

The Emergence of the Classical Gold Standard in the 1870s

At this point, it is instructive to consider how the classical gold standard came into existence in the 1870s. Consider that, following the various European revolutions of the 1840s and 1850s and the Franco-Prussian war of 1871, the European political landscape had been transformed. A new balance of power had been established on the continent. Economic hardship was giving way to an era of growth, trade, and integration.

There was, however, no dominant economic power, no hegemon to provide a reserve currency for all. The United Kingdom had a global empire and a formidable navy, to be sure, but its ability to project power, economic or otherwise, into the Baltic region or the interior of Eurasia was limited, as demonstrated by the growth of the Prussian-led, central European economic *Zollverein*[10] and, rather more painfully, by the Crimean War.

It was out of this nonhegemonic political environment, characterized by growing international trade, that the classical gold standard emerged. In other words, it arose from the bottom up, rather than being imposed from the top down. Gold provided an objective, universal reference point for cross-border trade between countries that were once and future adversaries. Indeed, as one prominent study of the classical gold standard puts it:

> [T]he regime dynamics of the classical gold standard were founded on neither cooperation nor hegemonic leadership.

---

[10] *Zollverein* translates into English as "customs union." As Prussia grew in size, it began to act as a regional economic hegemon, imposing a form of mercantilism on its neighbors within the Zollverein. Interestingly, it was Prussia, rather than Great Britain, that began to rely more exclusively on gold, rather than silver, in the years leading up to the classical gold standard.

Both the origin and stability of the gold standard, in fact, resulted from much more diffuse or decentralized processes (i.e., not managed at the international level). . . .

Contrary to many visions of the gold standard, the regime dynamics upon which it was founded showed a strongly diffuse character. Moreover, the managerial elements that did show up were quite different from the conventional visions of hegemony and cooperation in the literature on international regimes. The nature of hegemony was much more unintentional and non-state than prevailing theories of hegemonic regimes can account for. . . .

Cooperation, too, fails to explain the origin and stability of the regime. In fact, **it was a failure to cooperate that led to the emergence of the regime in the 1870s**. . . . Moreover, it is not clear that more cooperation would have produced a more stable regime. The lack of cooperative schemes effectively limited the degree to which authorities could allow their macroeconomies to arrive at conditions that would have threatened convertibility (i.e., moral hazard and adverse substitution leading to inflation and fiscal deficits. . . .

In sum, the gold standard showed very little cooperation among national governments in the process of formal regime building. **The rise of the gold standard can be seen more as a case of a regime emerging from the failure to cooperate.** (Emphasis added.)[11]

There are thus strong parallels between the 1870s and today. The United States began to lose hegemonic status in the 1960s, to which the outflow of gold and the gradual decline in the U.S. share of global economic output attest. The closing of the gold window in 1971 was an important signpost in this regard. More recently, the fiat-dollar standard has demonstrably destabilized the global economy and led to a series of escalating monetary and currency disputes. The global economy is in desperate need of a new, more stable monetary order, yet it must be one that can function absent a hegemon and without an established, institutionalized basis for cooperation.

[11] Guilio Gallarotti, *The Anatomy of an International Monetary Regime: The Classical Gold Standard 1880–1914* (New York: Oxford University Press, 1995), 218–227.

Back in 1997, over a decade before the 2008–2009 global credit crisis, Nobel laureate Robert Mundell observed that:

> We can look upon the period of the gold standard . . . as being a period that was unique in history, when there was a balance among the powers and no single superpower dominated.[12]

As it now appears, the "balance among the powers" to which Mundell refers may not be so unique after all. The stage for gold has been set.

[12]Robert Mundell, "The International Monetary System in the 21st Century: Could Gold Make a Comeback?" Lecture delivered at St. Vincent College, Letrobe, Pennsylvania, March 12, 1997.

CHAPTER 6

The Inevitability of Regime Change

The seven problems of the present international monetary
system . . . are all related to the change in the role of the dollar.
—Nobel laureate Robert Mundell,
presentation to the China G-20 Seminar,
March 31, 2011

Although textbooks may view gold as the old money, markets
are using gold as an alternative monetary asset today.
—World Bank President Robert Zoellick, 2010

That which can't go on, won't. The fiat dollar standard has destabilized the global economy to such a degree that regime change has
become inevitable. With no other viable alternative, absent hegemonic or established institutional order, gold is going to resume its
historical place at the center of the global monetary system. It is only
a matter of time. Indeed, as we will see in Part II, the movement
away from the dollar and towards gold has already begun.

A gold standard solves the fundamental global problem of excessive, unsustainable money and credit growth because the supply of
reserves becomes essentially finite. You can't print gold, no matter
how much a government might wish to. Gold is expensive to produce.
You dig more out of the ground only when the price is high enough
to justify this diversion of productive economic resources. And what
drives the price higher in the first place? Why, excessive fiat money

and credit growth! As such, the gold standard is self-regulating. It requires neither a hegemon nor an established institutional order to impose it. Indeed, as we have just seen in the prior chapter, the classical gold standard arose due to a relative absence of international cooperation in monetary affairs.

Why Gold? Why Can't Other Commodities Provide the Basis for International Money?

Those not familiar with the classical gold standard and the role of gold as a universal money in general throughout history frequently wonder why gold, in particular, has been the preferred monetary asset. In fact, as it happens, silver has been more commonly used as money, but for smaller, day-to-day transactions and for intranational rather than international trade. Copper, nickel, and other metals have also been used for everyday transactions and, in many countries, still provide the material for modern coinage. Yet cross-border commerce and balance-of-payments have been dominated by gold. Why should that be so?

First, as mankind has always placed a much higher valuation on gold than on silver, due most probably to its relative scarcity, it is more practical for use in large transactions, which cross-border balance of payments tend to be.

Second, gold has essentially zero industrial uses. Indeed, due to its relatively high malleability, gold has been used in religious art and artifacts or as decorative jewelry more commonly than as bullion, a relatively modern invention by comparison. Silver and other precious metals have a broad and growing range of practical industrial uses, which greatly affects the available stocks, whereas the world's stock of gold tends to remain relatively constant, growing only slowly over time. This stability of the stock is essential for money. A money with an unstable, unpredictable supply simply can't function as such, as we have already seen in our discussion of why the fiat dollar is losing its preeminent global reserve status.

Third, gold is easily distinguishable from other metals. While platinum is rarer, it can be difficult to distinguish from both palladium and silver. Gold is the only yellow metal.

This combination of gold's unique color, ease of malleability, and relative scarcity is simply not shared by any other metal, nor any commodity substance yet discovered. Gold thus stands alone as the international money standard *par excellence*. There is also the non-trivial matter of historical and cultural precedent which, in certain parts of the world, borders on the religious.

That said, there is a case to be made that for specialized, relatively non-diversified, exporting economies, producing primarily commodities, be they metals, or energy, or agricultural products, the most appropriate money, or valuation benchmark for their exchange rates versus other currencies, could be that which they produce for export. Much work has been done in this area by Jeffrey Frankel of Harvard University.

For the world economy as a whole, however, which is not specialized but rather highly diversified, the only commodity that can credibly claim universal acceptance as money is that which always has, throughout history. Agrarian, artisanal, preindustrial, industrial, and, as demonstrated today, even postindustrial societies have always found gold to possess a unique role as a store of value and, by extension, as a universal money.

The late Roy Jastram opined in his classic work, *The Golden Constant,* that perhaps the most fundamental reasons that gold has held its preeminent monetary place throughout world history ultimately are derived from human emotion. On the one hand, gold is regarded as simply beautiful, perhaps because it is the only metal the color of the sun, the source of all light and life. On the other, even though it provides no physical nourishment, warmth, or shelter, it gives mankind comfort in times of stress or distress. No government-mandated legal tender can possibly replace that which transcends all government, all laws, and, indeed, all things created by man.

Gold Provides a Practical, Off-the-Shelf Solution to the Problems Created by Modern Central Banking

As for central banking, the problems associated with arbitrary interest rate manipulation and inflation targeting disappear when gold takes center stage. The gold standard cares not what the rate of consumer price inflation is. It cares only about the amount of money and credit circulating in the economy. If too much is circulating, the price of gold rises, sucking it back in. If too little, the price of gold falls, releasing more. Yes, under a gold standard, policy makers largely lose control of the money supply, but that is precisely the point. You don't fix a broken global monetary equilibrium by giving policy makers the power to micromanage it to their own arbitrary, nationalistic ends. Rather, you start over, with an objective reference point that restores confidence precisely because it cannot be manipulated by any one party or group of parties to their benefit at the expense of others. That objective reference point is gold.

This important point has been emphasized by none other than Robert Zoellick, president of the World Bank. In a provocative editorial published in the *Financial Times* in November 2010, he listed a range of actions that should be taken to help stabilize the global financial system. One of these was to reinstate gold as a universal monetary reference point. Following a discussion of how a number of major currencies, taken together, could form the basis for a new global monetary system, he wrote that:

> The system should also consider employing gold as an international reference point of market expectations about inflation, deflation and future currency values.[1]

In the article, he concluded his discussion of a future role for gold by addressing critics of the idea, pointing out that some may regard gold as "old money" but that the present, stark reality was that gold was clearly now regarded by financial markets as an "alternative monetary asset."

There are other ways in which a return to gold can restore confidence in the global monetary system. Perhaps the simplest is to consider a few empirical observations: Gold did not cause the great credit crisis of 2008, from which the global economy has yet to properly recover. Gold is not causing the surge in price inflation across most of the developing world. Gold did not destabilize the global monetary system; the fiat dollar did. And for those with a bit more historical perspective, it was while on a gold standard that the Western world's standard of living effectively quintupled in just a few generations. The idea that a gold standard is incompatible with strong, sustainable economic growth is hogwash; the truth is quite the opposite.

There are those who argue, wrongly, that had the world been on a gold standard, the great credit crisis of 2008 would have been even worse, as policy makers' hands would have been tied. But that is precisely the point. Let's put the horse in front of the cart where it belongs: Had their hands been tied, and the excessive money and credit growth of recent decades thereby restrained, a crisis of systemic proportions would never have materialized in the first place.

---

[1] Robert Zoellick, "The G20 Must Look beyond Bretton Woods II," *Financial Times*, November 7, 2010.

As with Bretton Woods, Bretton Woods II was a stable equilibrium only to the extent that the various participants were willing to confer the benefit of lower borrowing costs on the United States in return for global monetary stability and, it was assumed, sustainable rates of healthy, noninflationary economic growth. The global credit crisis has shown this apparently beneficial quid pro quo to have been a mirage. Whereas the last time the world faced a similar situation, in 1971, the United States resolved the issue by unilaterally severing the dollar's link to gold, this time round, the only resolution is for the global economy to sever its link to the fiat dollar reserve standard.

More specifically, Bretton Woods II, like Bretton Woods, was unsustainable because of the exorbitant privilege of the United States: It's ability to print the global reserve currency. Thus exposed by the Federal Reserve's serial unconventional monetary measures (e.g., QE1, QE2, etc.) for all to see, the major global economic players now have no incentive to perpetuate a demonstrably flawed system, other than to avoid the disruption that would accompany the movement to a new global monetary equilibrium providing a stable alternative to the fiat dollar. But as we shall see, there is a growing body of evidence that, in fact, the groundwork is already being laid behind the scenes for a move away from the fiat-dollar standard toward something else. And, not surprisingly for those who have bothered to take even a cursory look at economic history, that something is gold. In Part II, we turn to the topic of what the transition back to gold will most probably look like and explore a variety of possible scenarios.

PART

II

Running the Golden Gauntlet: Transition Scenarios Back to a Gold Standard

> I now believe that the United States will return to some form
> of a gold standard within the next five years.
>
> —Steve Forbes, April 2011

In Part I, we determined that the fiat dollar standard equilibrium, destabilized by the global credit crisis, is now collapsing. But the monetary disorder associated with the fiat dollar standard, which became glaringly and painfully obvious to all beginning in 2008, cannot be resolved by moving to just another fiat money standard. There is no currency that can, all at once, replace the dollar with sufficient confidence, objectivity, and trust. While the euro might be the leading candidate, the euro area has increasingly evident underlying economic problems, and many European leaders would not welcome the currency strength that would be necessarily associated with euro reserve currency status. The yen's days as a challenger to the dollar are long gone. The Chinese yuan, although a potential future candidate, lacks sufficient deep, liquid, and reliable financial markets and, indeed, fundamental legal foundations to take the role.

The special drawing right (SDR), as a basket of currencies, is even more problematic. This is due primarily to the degree of institutional cooperation and trust required to construct and maintain a global monetary regime that requires the active cooperation of a critical mass of its members in both monetary and fiscal matters. As seen in the final chapter of Part I, such cooperation today is unlikely, as U.S. economic priorities so clearly diverge from those of most other countries, with the possible exception of Japan. As we have also seen in Part I, the classical gold standard came into existence not because of international cooperation and trust but rather an absence of it, just as we observe today.

While this is perhaps obvious to those who bother to examine the cycles of economic history and how periods of monetary and credit boom and bust invariably lead back to gold, the modern economic mainstream, reared on a fiat currency diet, fails to acknowledge this fundamental economic and historical reality. One argument often directed at those advocating or predicting a return to some form of gold standard is that it would simply be too disruptive and destructive to the global economy. But this is like arguing that war, the most disruptive and destructive of all human endeavors, will never happen.

We know such reasoning is superficial and misleading. Wars tend to commence when one or more countries become aggressive, desperate, or some combination of the two. The same is true for major changes to official monetary arrangements. Rising powers seeking to grow their economic clout will do what is necessary to gain access to markets, including establishing credibility for their currency or coinage. Fading powers will resist the loss of such credibility, although they may find that their domestic economic objectives come into conflict with regime maintenance, just as the United States did in 1971. And of course, financial markets will adjust asset prices, interest, and exchange rates as necessary to reflect the ever-shifting risks present in the global economy.

As the twentieth century drew to a close, it was increasingly evident to informed observers, including many economists, historians, and so-called futurists, that U.S. global influence—economic, political, perhaps even military—had begun to fade. The U.S. share of the global economy, nearly 50 percent at the conclusion of World War II, had slipped to less than 25 percent. Moreover, the United States had become a large net debtor to the rest of the world, implying an accelerating transfer of relative wealth and economic power in the future.

Partly as a consequence, U.S. diplomatic influence began to decline in most parts of the world, as regional powers grew gradually more assertive. In Europe, a new, single currency, the euro, challenged the dollar's nearly exclusive reserve currency status. Russia had begun to emerge from a prolonged slump during which obsolete Communist-era industries were restructured and modernized. China had begun to reap the benefits of widespread market-based reforms initiated by Deng Xiaoping more than a decade earlier and was exerting growing influence throughout Asia and around the world. Rival power India was also taking steps in this direction. In South America, the regional giant Brazil finally began to get its economic act together.

By the mid-2000s, the rising powers of Brazil, Russia, India, and China—colloquially known as the BRICs—began to officially recognize their rising power status by holding annual summits to discuss how best to advance their increasingly common interests. In spring 2011, at a summit meeting held on Hainan Island in the South China Sea, to which South Africa, a major gold producer, was also invited, the BRICs made a formal statement that, in key respects, echoed the bombshell comments made by Charles de Gaulle in February 1965:

> Recognizing that the international financial crisis has exposed the inadequacies and deficiencies of the existing international monetary and financial system, we support the reform and improvement of the international monetary system, with a broad-based international reserve currency system providing stability and certainty.[1]

Unlike de Gaulle, who made explicit reference to gold in his famous remarks, the BRICs instead mentioned the potential role of the SDR—the International Monetary Fund currency basket index—in the Sanya summit declaration, but the implication was nevertheless clear: The rising economic powers were calling for an alternative to the fiat dollar as the preeminent reserve currency.

And so, the monetary reform genie has been released from the bottle. The global economy, of which the United States has for decades been a declining part, has clearly embarked on the transition away from the fiat dollar reserve standard that has been in place since August 1971.

---

[1]This is point 16 of the Sanya Declaration, BRICS Leaders Meeting (with South Africa as a special guest), Sanya, Hainan, China, April 14, 2011.

Lacking both a national fiat currency alternative and also the requisite cooperation to move toward the global SDR currency basket standard, as discussed in Part I, it becomes rather clearer what sort of regime is going to replace the fiat dollar, at least for a period of time during which the global financial system deleverages, rebalances and heals itself: some form of gold standard.

In this part, we consider what this transition might look like. It could be rather orderly, in particular if the United States decides to take the initiative to return to gold rather than allow itself to be overtaken by events. However, if history is any guide, it is unlikely that the United States will have the foresight to initiate a fundamental reform of the global monetary order and ease the transition away from the fiat dollar on its own, thereby relinquishing unilaterally its long-held extraordinary privilege. More likely is an unpredictable, crisis-driven, disorderly, even dangerous process, similar, indeed, to that from which the fiat dollar emerged in the first place.

What Kind of a Gold Standard?

While an important topic to be sure, a detailed discussion of exactly what type of gold standard is likely to succeed the fiat dollar standard is beyond the scope of this book. A key point that will be made in Part II is that a gold standard must be credible to be sustainable. Credibility can take any number of specific forms but there must be clear rules regarding how gold is to be exchanged between countries and under what circumstances.

Under Bretton Woods, for example, gold was exchanged periodically but, rather than ship physical gold from country to country, a costly and time consuming exercise, balance of payments adjustments normally were made by moving bullion from one country's locker to another's in the basement vault below the NY Federal Reserve building in lower Manhattan. France's decision to take physical custody of a sizeable portion of its gold by shipping it back home was the exception, rather than the rule, although it was permitted. Had it not been, Bretton Woods would not have been as credible.

Other factors equal, the fewer the links in the monetary chain between actual transactions, public or private, and the legal and physical transfer of gold, the more credible the regime is likely to be. How much credibility is required is a function of trust. The more countries trust one another, the more tolerant they will be of extraterritorial custody or other conventions of convenience.

Under the classical gold standard in the late nineteenth and early twentieth centuries, there were considerably more frequent transfers of physical gold between countries than under Bretton Woods, in large part because national central banks or even commercial banks were required by domestic law to provide gold on demand in exchange for banknotes. (Indeed, banknotes originated as warehouse receipts for stored gold, prior to their adoption for use as money.)

Some critics of the gold standard point out how prohibitively cumbersome it would be, in the modern world of electronic banking, to return to a full gold standard under which physical transfers were required. But this argument is specious. There is no difference in principle between electronic banking referencing pieces of paper—as is currently the case—and electronic banking referencing ounces of gold, or fractions thereof. Indeed, the better argument is to point out that modern technology theoretically makes it substantially *less* cumbersome to operate a gold standard and thereby avoid the perennial pitfalls associated with unbacked, fiat currencies.

CHAPTER

7

A Golden Bolt out of the Blue

For an enemy that cannot match the United States on the land, sea or air, we estimate that the temptation to fight in the financial markets is great. Our financial markets are more vulnerable than ever, the methods for attacking them are easy and inexpensive, and the returns to the enemy in terms of the destruction of wealth and confidence are inestimable. It is imprudent to take this threat lightly or ignore it. There will be no time to prepare once financial warfare commences.

—James G. Rickards, Senior MD, Omnis Group Inc.

*I*magine if you will the following scenario, set in August 2013:

It was a fine summer evening at Camp David, warm and clear. The president's key cabinet members and policy advisers were assembling in the Presidents Lounge of Aspen Cabin. They had come from all over, not only Washington. The Treasury secretary had been in New York overseeing attempts by the New York Fed to restore confidence in financial markets. The secretary of State had been in Brazil trying to ease growing trade tensions. The Defense secretary had been in Taiwan trying to reassure that tiny, vulnerable ally that the United States could still defend it against an increasingly powerful and assertive China. And the National Security adviser had been in London, attending a conference at the Royal Institute for International Affairs.

It had been over 40 years since a similar emergency gathering had been hastily arranged, at the request of President Nixon, in that case to discuss policy options for responding to an international run on the U.S. gold stock. This time around, things were both similar yet different. While there was no run on the gold stock—the United States was, of course, no longer on a gold exchange standard—there sure was out of the dollar.

Just two days earlier, Russia had made a sudden and shocking policy announcement that it was introducing a new global currency, the "dolar", which would be fully convertible into gold at a fixed rate of 1 dolar per kilogram. Russia had been accumulating gold reserves for some time, although precisely how much was a closely guarded state secret. Clearly, they now believed they had accumulated a sufficiently large gold reserve to credibly back this new currency at a level close to the prevailing market rate.

To bolster the attractiveness of this new currency, Russia took the additional step of easing dolar-gold convertibility by allowing it to take place in the neutral locations of Zurich and Singapore. Moreover, the currency was to be administered by a bank in London, so financial markets would not need to work through the Russian banking system. Finally, English law was to prevail in any dispute over dolar contracts. Overnight, Russia thus presented the world with a liquid, convertible, gold-backed alternative to the unbacked fiat dollar reserve currency from which the world had been struggling to wean itself for several years.[1]

> The Central bank of the Russian Federation (Bank of Russia) Press release, Moscow, August 15, 2013
>
> The Central Bank of the Russian Federation (CBR) hereby announces the following facilities and processes which are in place and available for counterparty inquiry immediately:
>
> Point 1. CBR has arranged long-term use of vaults in Zurich and Singapore capable of holding up to 10,000 metric tonnes of gold. Security is provided by G4S and is state-of-the-art, including multiple security perimeters, biometric scanning, advanced encryption standard 264-bit encryption of communi-

[1]Jim Rickards posited this scenario back in 2009 at the Johns Hopkins Advanced Physics Laboratory Unrestricted Warfare Symposium, as documented in the published proceedings, which includes the mock Russian press release reprinted with permission here. I thank him for permission to use this scenario, which he also includes in his new book, *Currency Wars* (New York: Penguin Group, 2011).

cations channels, blast-proof construction, and redundant power supplies. CBR has moved the gold component of the Russian Federation international reserves to these vaults amounting to approximately 500 metric tonnes.

Point 2. CBR announces the issuance of the Gold Reserve Dolar (GRD) to be issued in book-entry form by the Global Dolar Bank plc in London (SWIFT: GDBAGB) acting as fiscal agent of CBR. One GRD is equal to one kilogram of pure gold (the Fixed Conversion Rate, or FC Rate). The GRD is freely convertible into gold at the FC Rate and is freely transferable to any designated party on the books of the Global Dolar Bank or any other approved bank maintaining GRD accounts. CBR invites creditworthy and prudently regulated banks worldwide to open GRD accounts and facilities on their books that can be cleared on a real-time gross settlements basis via Global Dolar Bank. The Global Dolar Bank clearance, settlement, and accounts systems are operated on IBM Blade Servers using Logica CAS++ payments solution software.

Point 3. The Gold Reserve Dolar may be acquired in any quantity by delivery of the appropriate amount of gold at the FC Rate to any one of the vaults noted in Point 1. Upon receipt of good delivery, the pertinent number of GRDs will be credited to the delivering party's account at Global Dolar Bank. Gold Reserve Dolars are freely redeemable into gold in any quantity by instruction to Global Dolar Bank and by providing delivery instructions to one of the vaults.

Point 4. All matters pertaining to title, transfer and operation of GRDs and Global Dolar Bank plc are determined solely under English law and heard exclusively in English courts. All matters pertaining to physical possession, delivery and receipt of gold in the vaults will also be determined solely under English law and may be heard either in English courts or courts located in Switzerland and Singapore respectively. Opinions of law from Queen's Counsel and leading counsel in Switzerland and Singapore respectively are available for inspection.

Point 5. Effective immediately, all sales of Russian exports may be negotiated, denominated and paid for in GRDs only. The existing Russian Ruble will continue to be legal tender for domestic transactions conducted solely by parties within the Russian Federation.

Point 6. Effective immediately CBR announces a tender for unlimited quantities of gold. Any gold tendered under this facility will be paid for by delivery to the seller of U.S. Treasury bills, notes or bonds at an exchange value calculated by reference to the market value of securities determined in USD closing prices on Bloomberg and the market value of gold determined in USD by the London fixing, both for the average of the three business days immediately preceding the settlement date of the exchange.

Point 7. CBR will provide GRD lending facilities and GRD swap lines via Global Dolar Bank plc for approved counterparties with eligible collateral as determined in the sole discretion of CBR.

End of press release.

While it was impossible to know exactly how this decision had come about—not one of the various U.S. intelligence agencies had warned the president or relevant members of Congress of the possibility—it was understandable, given the context, that Russia was willing to confront the United States in this way. Not only was the United States provoking a potentially nuclear Iran into a military confrontation that could quite easily draw in Asian nuclear powers, such as Pakistan and India, but also Iran was an important trading partner for Russia. The dangers to Russia, economic and military, were simply too close to home.

And so it was, amid the growing threat of another Mideast war, rising oil prices, and a chronically weak, stagflationary U.S. economy, that by making the ruble convertible into gold, Russia sparked a global run out of the U.S. dollar and, by extension, U.S. financial markets and the banking system.

The New York Fed was in the front line. As central banks around the world began to sell a portion of their holdings of U.S. Treasury bonds in exchange for the preferred new alternative of gold-backed, dolar-denominated securities, interest rates rose sharply. Naturally, the Fed responded to this unwelcome development by creating more reserves, but, while this did maintain a degree of liquidity in the banking system, it had a devastating effect on the U.S. dollar. Now that there was a credible, gold-backed alternative to the dollar, the injection of fresh reserves had a direct, immediate impact on the dollar's value in the foreign exchange markets. Banks were taking their fresh dollar reserves and exchanging them for dolars, euros, yen, Swiss francs; the point was to try and minimize their exposure to the recently deposed fiat dollar reserve currency.

Within 24 hours, the dollar lost some 20 percent of its value in broad, trade-weighted terms. Oil, gold, and other commodity prices soared by even more as global investors fled into liquid real assets, anticipating shockwaves throughout the global financial system.

The president's advisers made it clear that he needed to take immediate, probably rather bold action, if a full-scale U.S. financial market meltdown was to be averted. The dollar might have just lost its preeminent global reserve status, to be sure, something that could not be restored by executive order or legislative action. But there were still things that would need to be done to stabilize the home front and avoid a level of domestic economic chaos that, if not dealt with effectively, might morph into political chaos before long.

Déjà Vu: Dollar Crisis Meeting at Camp David, 42 Years Later

Having reached a quorum by just after 6 P.M., the president entered the lounge, welcomed the attendees, and briefly explained his appreciation for the gravity of the situation. He then handed the floor over to the Treasury secretary, who was tasked, much as his predecessor John Connally had been more than 40 years earlier, with crafting some plan whereby confidence in the U.S. dollar, financial markets, and banking system could be quickly restored.

"Thank you, Mr. President," the secretary began. "We appreciate that this is the greatest crisis of your presidency and probably the greatest economic policy challenge faced by any administration since at least President Nixon and possibly even FDR.

"Before we begin our discussion, I have asked the undersecretary for Monetary Affairs to provide some background on recent events."

"Thank you, Mr. Secretary," he began. "Global financial markets have been jittery for weeks due to growing concerns of a U.S.-Russian showdown over Iran, which recently formally announced that it had acquired an intermediate-range ballistic missile capability to augment its presumed nuclear bomb development program with a proven delivery mechanism. As you all know, we took the decision to push for the UN to apply immediate sanctions on Iran via the UN Security Council, prohibiting any and all trade with Iran. However, we were met with stiff, immediate, coordinated public resistance by

Russia and China, who expressed their joint preference to negotiate a treaty with Iran that would limit the size and scope of Iran's future nuclear ambitions to primarily defensive purposes. Among other reasons, they mentioned that Pakistan and Israel, both nuclear powers, were in the front line vis-à-vis Iran and easily within range of its new missiles. Russia and China believe strongly that this, combined with their own, massive retaliatory capabilities and modest IRBM interception capabilities, will deter Iran from ever using nuclear weapons for offensive purposes. As such, they believe that such a treaty would be effective and thereby would obviate the need for damaging economic sanctions.

"While here in the U.S. we are accustomed to sanctions on Iran, which have been in place in some form since 1979, this cannot be said of either Russia or China. They have only ever supported sanctions on Iran when the United States declared it was of a critical national interest, most recently to prevent Iran acquiring a nuclear capability. Now that Iran is as far down the road as it is, neither Russia nor China sees any logic in continuing to impose sanctions, much less expand them. Indeed, China and Iran are in negotiations at this very moment regarding the upgrading of an Arabian Sea container port facility and associated rail and transport links in southeastern Iran.

"Turning now to the economy, the tensions associated with the inevitable arrival of the 'Persian Bomb' have sent oil prices sharply higher, to the detriment of financial market sentiment. It doesn't help matters that the economy has still failed to recover properly from the prolonged slump that began in 2008, notwithstanding heroic amounts of fiscal and monetary stimulus, including most recently the Fed's QE4 policy of corporate bond spread targeting.

"Abroad, economically destabilizing rates of inflation have been afflicting many countries, including all four of the BRICs. They argue that this is the inevitable consequence of U.S. Federal Reserve policy. As you well know, we disagree. All they have ever needed to do is to allow their currencies to appreciate. With this action by Russia, which implies a stronger ruble, we are also already seeing the other BRICs currencies appreciating."

At this point, the president interjected, "You mean that the dollar is depreciating, of course. And don't forget that it has been our policy since at least 2004 that China and certain other countries should allow their currencies to appreciate more substantially."

"Well, yes, there are two sides to any exchange rate. And yes, that has been our policy."

"Not entirely," continued the president. "What I mean is that the dollar is depreciating not only relative to other currencies but also in absolute, purchasing-power terms. Look at oil and gasoline. Look at wheat and corn. My God, look at cotton! Was this our policy, too?"

The president glared over at his Treasury secretary, visibly annoyed with the undersecretary. "Yes, Mr. President," the undersecretary continued in a less certain voice, "the dollar is depreciating. Hence the upward pressure not only on commodity prices but also on interest rates, which threatens the solvency of our banking system, our ability to service our national debt, and the health of our economy in general."

"Quite. Now we have expressed for years our desire that the BRICs, in particular China, would allow their currencies to appreciate. Well, Goddammit, now they're doing it, and look at the result! How are we going to explain to the American public that a policy that we have been pushing for years is now threatening us with the second banking crisis in less than a decade!"

"Please, Mr. President," interrupted a defensive Treasury secretary. "We never pushed for Russia or any other country, for that matter, to suddenly make its currency convertible into gold."

Now the director of National Intelligence chimed in. "Mr. President, I can assure you that none of the U.S. intelligence agencies anticipated this, nor could they have. There was no evidence of such planning received by the NSA or from anywhere else in the broad intelligence apparatus."

"Excuse me," interrupted the president, "has it not occurred to you that although Russia may have chosen the precise timing of this action, there is clear and present evidence that the other BRICs were fully prepared for this? Haven't you noticed that their currencies have all risen by a comparable amount versus the dollar? This looks like a coordinated action!"

"We all know—indeed, we are among those who criticized them at the time—that the U.S. intelligence community completely failed to anticipate the rapid implosion of the Soviet Union in the early 1990s. Well, at least that was a failure to anticipate developments in a single, albeit highly secretive country. Now, we have a failure to properly identify that any one of four countries, including two we have supposedly penetrated to the highest levels of government, have spent at least a number of months and more probably a number of years planning the greatest global economic policy coup in, well, in centuries! How am I supposed to explain that to the American people?"

The room fell silent. No one knew how to respond or had the courage to do so. The president was right. The United States had not only completely failed to anticipate a major Russian economic and monetary policy shift, clearly supported by the other BRICs and who knows who else, that threatened the U.S. financial system and economy, but also the United States was, suddenly and glaringly obviously, economically and politically isolated. Russia might be in the lead at this particular moment, but the bulk of U.S. major trading partners were clearly in the convoy.

The president continued: "Now gentlemen. We need to restore confidence in our currency, in our financial markets, in our banking system, and in our economy. And we need to do so right now. Before Monday morning in Asia, when financial markets reopen, I am going to make the announcement that accomplishes all of these things. You lot are going to craft it. I want a draft on my desk by 6 A.M. tomorrow morning. Mr. Secretary, you are in charge. Good night."

The president departed the lounge. Everyone stood aghast. They had never seen the president so angry. But then the president had never faced a crisis of this magnitude. While there were certain parallels to August 1971 and 1933, there were also differences, the most important of which was that the government was far larger now, relative to the economy, and thus so was the associated tax and financing burden. The population was older, with far more recipients of Social Security, Medicare, and other such programs introduced in prior decades amid less challenging demographics. Global military commitments, including the wars in Afghanistan, Pakistan, Libya, Somalia, Yemen, and Iraq and major policing actions elsewhere, were claiming by far the largest share of the federal budget since the Vietnam War. The trade balance was negative, not only because the United States imported most of its oil but also because most manufacturing now took place in more competitive economies abroad. And with the economy so weak, not only was defense a burden: Jobless benefits, food stamps, and other such counter-cyclical financial assistance programs were taking up a record portion of the federal budget. Moreover, chaos in state and local government finances was resulting in a huge reduction of those services and a growing risk that, at some point, the federal government might need to step in and provide certain guarantees to restore some degree of stability in the market for state and municipal borrowing. While each of these factors alone posed a major economic challenge, taken together they implied that the US was simply no longer in a dominant economic position globally, able to dictate terms in monetary matters.

No one really knew where to begin. But then the deputy director of the CIA spoke.

"You may not believe this, but we sorta 'war-gamed' this scenario back in 2009. It didn't go anywhere, not that I'm aware of. Not enough people took it as a serious threat. But we did war-game it and I recall roughly how it was resolved."

"How?" asked an astonished Treasury secretary, who indicated that he was prepared to retake the floor.

"Well, in brief, we restored gold convertibility."

"You mean as under Bretton Woods?"

"More or less. But mind you that we did so at a far higher gold price, to reduce the debt burden to a manageable level that restored a degree of global confidence in our ability to service the debt, to stabilize the dollar, and, hence, to stabilize the U.S. financial system."

"We can't recommend such a course of action to the president."

"And why not?"

"It would be too sudden. Too disruptive. It would lead to a burst of inflation. It would require an immediate rationalization of government finances. It would be akin to reaching the debt ceiling. We all know how that almost sparked a dollar crisis back in 2011."

"Excuse me, but the crisis has already been sparked. This discussion is about how we respond. You heard the president. As far as he knows, we never war-gamed this scenario. But we did. And we resolved it. No one took it seriously then, but it has happened now. And so we have a potential road map. I strongly recommend that all of us familiarize ourselves with it. Mr. Secretary, with your permission, I will have the relevant documents sent to all present for their staffs' immediate consideration."

"Fine. Now we are going to need to present the president with at least two and preferably three proposals in total. It appears we may have one, however unpalatable. I want two more."

The room fell silent again.

"Mr. Secretary," the secretary of Defense said quietly, "the Department of Defense has also war-gamed something along these lines."

"Really? I can't believe I'm hearing now that multiple agencies of the federal government that has just been blindsided had in fact previously imagined and war-gamed just such a scenario. Whatever, it is too late to worry about that now. Well, then, how does your scenario play out?"

"Well, it doesn't result in a return to the gold standard. But I'm afraid it does lead to a major war with both Russia and China, with a high risk of going nuclear and, at a minimum, resulting in the loss of three carrier groups and several key military bases in the Pacific and Indian Oceans."

"I see. Would anyone else like to make a proposal?"

8

Golden Preparations

Money—capital—has a life of its own. It's a force of nature, like gravity. Like the oceans, it flows where it wants to flow. This whole thing with gold is inevitable, we're just going with the tide. The only question is whether you want to let it go like an unguided missile and raise hell, or whether you want to keep it in the hands of responsible people.

—Maxwell Emery, fictional financier, *Rollover*, 1981

Jim Rickards is not the first person to envision the general scenario described in the previous chapter, in which some nation, or group of nations, decides to divest its dollar reserves in favor of gold or a gold-backed alternative. Indeed, something right along these lines was turned into a screenplay and major motion picture back in 1981, a time when confidence in the dollar had been badly shaken by a prolonged period of U.S. economic underperformance and monetary policy misdeeds in the aftermath of the Bretton Woods breakdown. As we observed in Part 1, these culminated in the brief, parabolic rise in the gold price to $850 and a rise in U.S. Treasury bond yields to the unheard of level of over 15 percent amidst a sharp recession.

Rollover starred Kris Kristofferson as Hubbell Smith, a young, gifted financier and protégé to an elder financial statesman, Maxwell Emery, played by the late Hume Cronyn. Jane Fonda also starred, as Lee Winters, an ambitious young businesswoman and Hubbell's eventual love interest. Here is a plot summary, courtesy of the Internet Movie Database (IMDb):

> While working on an important international financing deal with Winters, Smith discovers Emery is moving money belonging to the Arabs into gold as a safe haven against potential losses if the dollar collapses. The Arabs are extremely worried that if anyone finds out their assets will vanish in a public panic as American currency becomes worthless.
>
> Winters also discovers the plot, and wants to change the terms of the financing deal in exchange for her silence; she has overheard part of Smith's conversation with Emery and mistakenly believes he was double-crossing her. A fake limo driver who is actually working for the Arab investors tries to kidnap her with the intent of killing her—as, it turns out, they did to her husband—to prevent her from disclosing what she knows, and when the attempt on her life fails, the Arabs panic and pull all of their money out of every bank in America, and possibly the entire world.
>
> The globe is gripped by panic and rioting occurs as people discover all of their money is now worthless. Emery is shown in his office—dead, an apparent suicide. The economic crisis paralyzes the world, but by spilling over boundaries between east and west blocs, and between developing and industrialized nations, it also unites the world in common cause. In the penultimate scene, workers at Borough National stand idle while listening to a report of the growing economic crisis. As the camera pans across the trading floor of the bank, the viewer sees that it's now empty of workers, the lights off, the desks and machines covered—completely inactive. Only Smith remains.

While in *Rollover* the instigators of a run on the dollar are the Arab oil-producing countries, rather than Russia, and their intention is not to crash the U.S. financial system, they nevertheless accidentally bring this about in their attempt to surreptitiously divest their dollar reserves and accumulate gold instead. As such, we have a scenario that, while perhaps best suited to Hollywood, is nevertheless worth contemplating. As Rickards puts it:

Notwithstanding an earlier period of globalization during 1880–1914, there can be little doubt that the current period of globalization from 1989–2009, beginning with the fall of the Soviet Union and the end of the Cold War, represents the highest degree of interconnectedness of the global system of finance, capital, and banking the world has ever seen. Despite obvious advantages in terms of global capital mobility facilitating productivity and the utilization of labor on an unprecedented scale, there are hidden dangers and second-order costs embedded in the sheer scale and complexity of the system. These costs have begun to be realized in the financial crisis that began in late 2007 and have continued until this writing and will continue beyond.

Among the emergent properties of this complexity are exponentially greater risks of catastrophic collapse leading to the complete insolvency of the global financial system. This dynamic has already begun to play out and will continue without the implementation of appropriate public policies, which, so far, are not in evidence.[1]

The point is that the existing, fiat-dollar-based global monetary system is both highly complex and inherently unstable. It could be undermined, deliberately or not, in any number of ways. We have already explored two hypothetical examples. There are more, including some that are perhaps more plausible. In this chapter, we consider how the United States, wary of losing the initiative to Russia, to other oil-producing nations, to China or to anyone else for that matter, might instead choose to prevent a disorderly return back to some form of gold standard by moving first, on its own initiative and terms. Indeed, this is precisely what Rickards proposes.

The U.S. could prevent this by preempting it—just by issuing a gold-backed dollar itself using the 4,600 metric tons available in Fort Knox (over nine times the Russian gold supply). Another approach is to convene a Bretton Woods II Conference,

---

[1]From the Unconstrained Warfare Symposium Proceedings, edited by Robert Lumin, Applied Physics Laboratory, School for Advanced International Studies, Johns Hopkins University, Baltimore, MD, 2009.

likely a G-20 meeting in today's world, and implement this on a global basis.[2]

As with many informed observers, Rickards understands that the fiat dollar cannot long remain the dominant global reserve currency due to the deteriorating U.S. fiscal and trade position and its economic underperformance relative to the rest of the world. It is, therefore, in its best interest to be the first mover and to minimize the associated disruption to the domestic and global economy.

Interestingly, back in the late 1980s, when the former Soviet Union was falling apart and the threat of an imminent hyperinflation and economic collapse loomed, two prominent U.S. economists, former Fed Governor Wayne Angell and Jude Wanniski, traveled to Leningrad (since renamed St. Petersburg) and Moscow and met with a number of Soviet economic and financial officials. They urged, among other measures, that the Soviets immediately move to shore up the rapidly devaluing ruble by backing it with their gold reserves. They also published this view in the U.S. financial press.[3] Back then, as now, the way to restore monetary stability is to restore credibility. What is good for the goose is, naturally, good for the gander. While the U.S. economy of today is not falling apart, nor has hyperinflation set in, its financial system is quite clearly dysfunctional, a problem with acute relevance for the entire world. Moving preemptively to restore credibility and, therefore, stability in global monetary affairs makes increasingly evident good sense.

Preparations for a Return to Gold Convertibility

Should the United States seek to take the initiative in restoring global monetary stability and eliminating the risk that the fiat dollar will be deposed in a disorderly fashion, there is a series of concrete steps that could be taken.

Most important is the acceptance of the fact that, at the current official accounting price of $42.50, a return to gold convertibility

[2]From the Unconstrained Warfare Symposium Proceedings, Applied Physics Laboratory, School for Advanced International Studies, Johns Hopkins University, Baltimore, MD, 2009.
[3]J. Wanniski, "Gold-Based Ruble? Two U.S. Economists Urge Hard Money on the Soviet Union," *Barron's*, September 25, 1989, 9; W. Angell (interview), "Put the Soviet Economy on Golden Rails," *Wall Street Journal*, October 5, 1989, A28.

would be hugely deflationary and most probably destroy the U.S. and, by extension global financial system in short order. Fortunately, history offers up a useful lesson for how *not* to restore gold convertibility, namely, the ultimately unsuccessful attempt by Great Britain to do so in 1925.

"The Economic Consequences of Mr. Churchill"

Winston Churchill was nothing if not resolute in his war and defense policies and politics, such as his program of naval modernization while first lord of the Admiralty, the disastrous Gallipoli campaign, the Blitz and Battle of Britain, the Harris bombing program of German cities, or his perennial unwillingness to contemplate the loss of the empire built with the blood, sweat, toil, and tears of the previous generations. But what was true of Churchill's policies in war was equally true in peace.

In 1925, convinced that there was no other appropriate policy choice, Churchill, while serving as chancellor of the Exchequer, placed the United Kingdom back onto the gold standard. Britain had suspended gold convertibility shortly after the outbreak of war in 1914 in order to facilitate war financing through inflation. But rather than consider the economic and monetary developments, including the inflation, that had taken place in the interim, he chose to restore gold convertibility at the pre–World War I parity. Never mind that World War I had been hugely expensive, that it had destroyed a good portion not just of the British but of the Continental European economy, that Germany and the other defeated powers had all recently experienced hyperinflationary currency crises, and, most important, that Britain itself had expanded the sterling monetary base dramatically in the years 1914 to 1925 such that, in restoring convertibility at the previous parity rate, a severe deflation and associated deep recession was assured.

Now it could be that Churchill and his advisers were unaware of the dangers of a severe deflation. After all, deflation in prices was the norm, rather than the exception, for much of the century leading up to World War I. Sterling had been fixed to gold, yet industrial productivity rose dramatically. With sterling stable but output rising, prices necessarily fell. This sort of deflation was not damaging; rather, it was entirely healthy. It also implied a gradual rise in living standards, as wages tended to remain more or less stable but, for any given wage, purchasing power steadily increased.

John Maynard Keynes was among those who warned of the dangers of restoring sterling to the pre–World War I convertibility rate. In his famous treatise, "The Economic Consequences of Mr Churchill," he writes satirically, as if he were advising the chancellor:

> Money-wages, the cost of living, and the prices which we are asking for our exports have not adjusted themselves to the improvement in the exchange, which the expectation of your restoring the Gold Standard, in accordance with your repeated declarations, has already brought about. They are about 10 per cent, too high. If, therefore, you fix the exchange at this gold parity, you must either gamble on a rise in gold prices abroad, which will induce foreigners to pay a higher gold price for our exports, or you are committing yourself to a policy of forcing down money wages and the cost of living to the necessary extent.
>
> We must warn you that this latter policy is not easy. It is certain to involve unemployment and industrial disputes. If, as some people think, real wages were already too high a year ago, that is all the worse, because the amount of the necessary wage reductions in terms of money will be all the greater.
>
> The gamble on a rise in gold prices abroad may quite likely succeed. But it is by no means certain, and you must be prepared for the other contingency. If you think that the advantages of the Gold Standard are so significant and so urgent that you are prepared to risk great unpopularity and to take stern administrative action in order to secure them, the course of events will probably be as follows.
>
> To begin with, there will be great depression in the export industries. This, in itself, will be helpful, since it will produce an atmosphere favourable to the reduction of wages. The cost of living will fall somewhat. This will be helpful too, because it will give you a good argument in favour of reducing wages.
>
> Nevertheless, the cost of living will not fall sufficiently and, consequently, the export industries will not be able to reduce their prices sufficiently, until wages have fallen in the sheltered industries. Now, wages will not fall in the sheltered industries, merely because there is unemployment in the unsheltered industries. Therefore, you will have to see to it that there is unemployment in the sheltered industries also. The way to do

this will be by credit restriction. By means of the restriction of credit by the Bank of England, you can deliberately intensify unemployment to any required degree, until wages do fall. When the process is complete the cost of living will have fallen too; and we shall then be, with luck, just where we were before we started.

We ought to warn you, though perhaps this is going a little outside our proper sphere, that it will not be safe politically to admit that you are intensifying unemployment deliberately in order to reduce wages. Thus you will have to ascribe what is happening to every conceivable cause except the true one. We estimate that about two years may elapse before it will be safe for you to utter in public one single word of truth. By that time you will either be out of office, or the adjustment, somehow or other, will have been carried through.[4]

Notwithstanding the objections of arguably the single most influential U.K. economist of the day, Churchill carried through his plans. Convertibility at the pre–World War I parity was restored. The result was an immediate and severe recession, soaring unemployment, wage deflation, and widespread industrial action and social unrest. By 1927, desperate for some assistance to shore up the ailing U.K. economy, Montagu Norman, governor of the Bank of England, traveled to New York to meet with the U.S. Federal Reserve Chairman, Benjamin Strong. He requested that the Fed help to ease the deflationary pressure on the U.K. economy by lowering interest rates temporarily to stimulate demand for U.K. exports to the United States. Thinking that such a policy was in the U.S. interest, Strong agreed.

The Roaring 20s were already well underway by 1927, but with the Fed's easing of monetary conditions, the roar entered a crescendo, taking the stock market and other asset prices to great heights. Leveraged speculators amassed fortunes in a matter of months. Many ordinary people who never before invested in the stock market entered the action in the hopes of making a quick buck. The party lasted for a good two years until, in October 1929,

---

[4]John M. Keynes, "The Economic Consequences of Mr. Churchill" (1925), 10–13, www.gold.org/government_affairs/gold_as_a_monetary_asset/historical_records _back_to_the_17th_century/the_heyday_of_the_gold_standard/.

amid overwhelming evidence that industrial production was in steep decline, the market crashed, and numerous overnight millionaires became overnight vagabonds. While it would take until 1931 to travel from Wall Street to Main Street, the Great Depression had begun.

Not coincidentally, it was in 1931 that the United Kingdom capitulated to the deflationary pressure of its decision to restore the pre-1914 sterling parity and went off the gold standard, never to properly return. As sterling devalued versus the dollar by 25 percent, the deflationary pressure was transmitted across the Atlantic to the United States, where it exacerbated the stress on the domestic banking system. In 1932, hundreds of U.S. banks failed. In 1933, the number of failures was even greater.

President Franklin Delano Roosevelt was convinced that something had to be done. It was unfair, of course, for the United Kingdom to try to pass on the deflationary consequences of its disastrous, botched return to sterling-gold convertibility to the United States. In 1934, he devalued the dollar by some 60 percent, although the United States remained on the gold standard. This was sufficient, however, to end the monetary and associated price deflation that had set in, beginning in 1929, and became particularly acute by 1932.

The Great Depression, of course, continued through the remainder of that decade and is not considered to have properly ended until the 1940s and World War II. But from 1934 onward the Great Depression was no longer a monetary, deflationary phenomenon. Rather, it was something else.

A Few Monetary and Other Lessons from the Great Depression

There is an extensive literature on the causes of the Great Depression, how policymakers responded, and how, eventually, the depression ended. There is, however, significant disagreement about all of these. The conventional wisdom, as presented by the Neo-Keynesian economic mainstream, is that the Great Depression was caused by the U.S. Federal Reserve, which failed to respond adequately to a sharp contraction in the domestic money supply that resulted from a severe drop in interbank lending. Milton Friedman and Anna Schwarz put forward this thesis in detail in their monumental study, *A Monetary History of the United States.* They believe that, had the Fed prevented a contraction of the money supply, the United States would have experienced only a severe recession, not a depression.[5]

The current leadership of the U.S. Federal Reserve, represented by Chairman Bernanke but also other Fed officials, subscribes to this view. As such, the Fed's response to the 2008 credit crisis and persistent economic weakness thereafter has been to ensure growth, or at a minimum, prevent a contraction in, the money supply, notwithstanding a severe contraction in interbank lending. This has left the U.S. banking system with a huge amount of so-called excess reserves: funds that could be lent out, but are not; instead they are left on deposit at the Fed, earning essentially zero interest.

In a way, these excess reserves act as a huge loan-loss reserve for the banking system. They may never be lent out. But they are liquid funds held in reserve that are available in the event that banks do need to draw on them, say, in the event of another funding crisis. While this huge pile of excess reserves may prevent bank insolvency indefinitely, their existence does not in any way force banks to lend. Nor does it encourage businesses to invest and create jobs. As such, by increasing excess reserves, the Fed could be perceived to be pushing on a string, to use a classic analogy. Another would be that you can lead a horse (bank) to water (liquidity), but you can't make him drink (lend).

Keynes suggested that the way to solve this problem was for the government to step in to replace the demand lost from the private sector by increasing spending, even though this would mean running a deficit. But Keynes believed that, in time, the economy would become self-sustaining again, and the government could then reduce spending and gradually pay down the accumulated debt. Neo-Keynesians point to U.S. deficit spending on WWII and the subsequent general economic recovery as a successful example of this policy.

There is, however, an alternative school of thought regarding what caused the Great Depression and why it eventually ended. According to this view, the Fed also caused the depression but did so already in the late 1920s, by creating an unsustainable investment boom with artificially low interest rates. This school understands the Roaring 20s as the ultimate cause of the Depression. The stock market and associated fixed investment boom represented a huge misallocation of resources facilitated by artificially low interest rates. But as with all such artificial booms, it was only a matter of time before, eventually, investors began to perceive that asset valuations were simply unsustainably high. As they began to cash out, a trickle quickly became a flood. The stock market crashed. Asset prices in general collapsed. Banks found that they were undercapitalized. As one loan after another went bad, banks began to fail.

According to this interpretation of the Great Depression, it would not have made a material difference to the broader economy had the Fed maintained a

(Continued)

[5]Anna Schwartz and Milton Friedman, *A Monetary History of the United States* (Princeton, NJ: Princeton University Press), 1963.

stable money supply or not. Any excess money would have simply sat around as excess reserves, just as it does today, with little if any impact on real economic activity, such as business investment and job creation.

But what of government? Amid a severe downturn, isn't it the government's job to step in and replace private-sector demand with increased government spending? After all, this is what Keynes recommended.

Let's consider again what happened in the Great Depression. The conventional wisdom holds that the government did not step in to provide stimulus until FDR took office in 1933 and that his various initiatives are what put a floor under the economy. Eventually, massive government spending associated with World War II is what ended the Depression once and for all.

Here, too, the alternative view is that, in fact, beginning already in 1930, President Hoover did all manner of things to try to stimulate the economy but, amid the massive investment bust, these measures were largely ineffective. Some commentators believe that they even made them worse. For example, Hoover was against wage cuts, believing that lower wages implied lower consumer demand and thus weaker growth. While that might be true, by discouraging companies from cutting wages, the result was higher unemployment than would otherwise have been the case. Yet regardless of whether fewer workers received higher wages, or more workers lower wages, in an investment bust, it was inevitable that growth would be weaker. As such, Hoover was partly responsible for the unusually high rate of unemployment from 1930 to 1933.

Once FDR took over, he expanded on what intervention Hoover had already been doing with increased government spending. Importantly, he also devalued the dollar by some 60 percent, which ended the price deflation associated with the early years of the depression and replaced it with moderate inflation. But growth remained weak, and unemployment remained high all through the 1930s, notwithstanding (or, perhaps, due to) a huge expansion of government in many sectors of the economy. By the early 1940s, the United States was at war and, yes, government spending soared. Many cite this as the reason that the depression finally ended. But guess what? As part of the war effort, workers were forced to accept sharply lower wages! Also overlooked is that the U.S. private savings rate soared in the 1940s as businesses and households paid down debt and rebuilt savings. Many households were more able to save as they now had two incomes, with women having entered the workforce en masse for the first time in U.S. history. In this view, it was not war spending that ended the depression; rather, it was a dramatic reduction in wages and a large increase in the savings rate, the very developments that were resisted by Presidents Hoover and Roosevelt from 1930 to 1939![6]

[6]A classic alternative view of the Great Depression is that of Austrian school economist Murray Rothbard, as presented in *America's Great Depression*, Fifth Edition (Auburn, AL: The Ludwig von Mises Institute, 2000).

Preparations for a U.S. Return to Dollar Convertibility

If the United States took the initiative and preemptively restored dollar convertibility, placing itself and, by implication, much of the world back on a gold standard, this would be far less disruptive to the current global financial system and also the U.S. economy specifically than it would be if the United States was in some way surprised and overtaken by the actions of others. That said, no economic policy change of that magnitude can go entirely smoothly, and, as with any major policy initiative, there would be winners and losers, notwithstanding that it best serves the national interest.

While it would certainly take an unusual degree of unity, vision, and leadership for a sitting U.S. president and Congress to take a step back from the incessant crisis fighting required by the faltering fiat dollar reserve standard and to consider rationally that it is in the best interest of the United States to be the first to move back to gold, we should hardly rule out that possibility. There are some in Congress and government generally who are supportive, most notably Representative Ron Paul (R) of Texas, and it does seem that their voices are being more widely heard at present than at any time since the Reagan Gold Commission studied the issue at length in the early 1980s. (Ron Paul, incidentally, was a member of that commission.)

As difficult a decision as it would be, were the United States to restore convertibility, how would it be likely to go about doing it? We have already pointed out what *not* to do, that is, try to restore convertibility at a previous, predevaluation rate, which in the case of the United States today would be $42.50, the rate prevailing on the day Nixon closed the gold window and allowed the fiat dollar to float. That would be so massively deflationary that it would almost certainly destroy the existing financial system, much to the detriment of the economy generally. More sensibly, the United States would restore convertibility at a rate that increased, rather than reduced, global confidence in the U.S. financial system and economy generally. This would imply a conversion rate that substantially reduces the U.S. real debt burden, public and private, to one that would be widely regarded as serviceable and thus sustainable by holders of dollars and dollar-denominated assets.

This goal would have to be balanced, however, against the rather obvious implied loss of purchasing power (price inflation) that would occur as a result of a large devaluation. Beyond a certain point, the devaluation would be so large that, while it would be economically sustainable in principle, it would be politically unpalatable in practice, as it would result in such a large surge in consumer price inflation that a substantial portion of the middle class would see their savings wiped out. This could well lead to widespread social unrest, which could damage rather than restore credibility in the ability of the United States to service its accumulated debts. (There might be other ways to assuage the potential social unrest, such as providing each citizen with a modest amount of gold, allowing each to participate favorably in a revaluation of gold, rather than merely suffer from a devaluation of the dollar. Intriguingly, the Chinese government encourages its citizens to accumulate both gold and silver as savings. The U.S. government should take note.)

What rate might best balance these two important concerns? There are several approaches to determining the ideal conversion rate. First, the United States could take the current, prevailing spot market rate, which would be hugely deflationary for the economy at large. Second, the United States could take a rate that adjusted for the growth in the monetary base since the gold window was closed. Third, the United States could return to a 40 percent money supply M0 coverage ratio, as per the Federal Reserve Act of 1913. Fourth, the United States could use a coverage ratio related to a broader monetary aggregate. Finally, the United States could choose a level high enough to imply a dramatic reduction of the current debt burden. While all but the first of these proposals would result in a sudden burst of inflation, they all nevertheless have the important benefit of containing future inflation expectations and stabilizing the dollar's value, as they would be seen as more sustainable and, hence, credible. And credibility is really the key to the entire exercise.

Historical Examples of Restoring Currency Credibility

Once lost, trust is difficult to regain. What is true at the personal level is also true at the social, national, and international levels. Yet as the size of the system grows, so does the difficulty. Indeed, it is precisely the relative lack of trust pervading the international system that makes it essential to have objective points of reference to maintain any degree of equilibrium, be it a recognized border between states or, when it comes to monetary affairs, an objective convention such as a credible gold standard.

While it is beyond the scope of this book to discuss it in any detail, there is always the chance that, whatever the transition to gold looks like, it becomes so disorderly that there is a wholesale run on the dollar and quite possibly also other fiat currencies, in favor of gold. If not addressed quickly with credible policies, a general run on fiat currencies could lead to a general global hyperinflation, which would be enormously destructive not only to the global economy but also to the very fabric of global society. If history is any guide, it is difficult to imagine that a general global hyperinflation would not result in at least one revolution and at least one war. More probably, it would result in several.

Should this occur, restoring currency credibility would be extraordinarily difficult. While in principle, restoring a monetary role for gold would be part of any viable solution, a broader range of policy actions would no doubt be required to make a gold standard credible. In this regard, it is instructive to look at past hyperinflations and how they were successfully brought under control.

A recent winner of the Nobel Memorial Prize in Economics, Thomas Sargent, did just this in a study some years ago. He looked at some of the twentieth century's most severe hyperinflations and examined the full range of policies that were implemented to try to restore currency stability. What he found, interestingly, was that quantitative factors, such as growth in the money supply, for example, were relatively less important than qualitative actions that demonstrated a clear commitment, on the part of policy makers, to restoring stable money.

Of particular importance was action on the fiscal side, due most probably to the fact that central banks, even those ostensibly highly independent, have historically come under enormous pressure to accommodate large government deficits with future, if not present, monetary expansion. As such, running a tight monetary policy alongside a highly expansionary fiscal policy is not considered a sustainable, credible situation. Action on the monetary front alone thus cannot end hyperinflation once it is under way. However, after there has been a clear, well-communicated swing back toward fiscal prudence, then monetary policy need not be highly restrictive, although it can help at the margin. As these changes in fiscal policy are necessarily large, they normally occur only after a change in government. At a minimum, there needs to be a change of leader and party. In more extreme cases, a revolution is necessary.

Hyperinflation, while naturally associated with high rates of money supply growth, is thus understood by Sargent to be more a fiscal than a monetary phenomenon, in terms of both how it begins and how it ends. I leave it to the reader to ponder what changes of government the admittedly remote risk of hyperinflation would imply for various countries today.[7]

---

[7] Thomas J. Sargent, "The Ends of Four Big Inflations," in Robert Hall, ed., *Inflation, Causes and Effects* (Chicago: University of Chicago Press, 1982).

The Current Spot Price

Let's consider these options in some detail. At the time of this writing, the price of gold has risen to around $1,700 per troy ounce. Naturally, that looks high in a historical comparison, as it is not only far above where the dollar left gold in 1971 at $42.50 but also not far from an all-time high. But let's place this price in its proper economic context. Adjusted by the U.S. Consumer Price Index, the price of gold at the 1980 peak was £2,340 in its 2011 equivalent, somewhat 40% higher than today. Looked at in a few other metrics, gold currently buys about as much crude oil as it did in 1971 and about as much wheat and about as much cotton. That is, the purchasing power of gold hasn't changed materially since 1971. What has changed, of course, is the purchasing power of the dollar, which has plummeted dramatically.

It may be difficult for readers to think this way, but consider: When you watch those classic TV shows about the United States in the nineteenth or early twentieth centuries, such as *Little House on the Prairie* or *The Waltons*, for example, many basic household goods were still priced in pennies rather than dollars. But does that really mean that things were less expensive back then? That somehow the standard of living was far higher? Of course not. Wages were also far lower. People had to work even longer to purchase a comparable basket of consumer goods. The standard of living was much lower than we enjoy today, notwithstanding the rather poor performance of the U.S. economy in recent years. Once again, what has changed is the purchasing power of the dollar, which is so much lower today than it was back then that it almost seems like a currency from another world.

By contrast, gold may seem a barbarous relic to some, but in my opinion, there is nothing barbarous about something that has more or less retained its purchasing power over the same time frame. Indeed, for those willing to look at the longer history of gold, through the centuries what becomes clear is that gold has done remarkably well at holding on to its purchasing power. War, famine, and revolution on the one hand or peace, prosperity, and stability on the other, gold has been the preserver of purchasing power par excellence.[8]

[8]The classic study on gold's remarkable ability to maintain its purchasing power over long periods of time, even those characterized by a broad variety of economic and political conditions, is *The Golden Constant* by Roy W. Jastram. Jill Leyland completed a revised edition of this 1970s study in 2007 for the World Gold Council.

Now some might argue that as gold is a zero-yield asset (slightly negative, in fact, considering storage costs), an investor would have forgone the interest available on dollars over this long time period. This is true. Dollars placed in the bank would have earned some interest. But of course, during the Great Depression, many banks failed, wiping out dollar depositors in the process. And ever since the Bretton Woods arrangements in 1944, the after-tax rate of interest on dollar deposits and T-bills has been insufficient to compensate the holders of dollars for the exponential loss of purchasing power they have suffered. During the 1970s, U.S. dollar real rates of interest were generally negative. The same has been the case since 2008. As such, cash is, in effect, a negative-yield asset.

There have been times, to be sure, when dollar interest rates were attractive, such as the early 1980s, for example. Indeed, high dollar interest rates were instrumental in ending the gold mania of the late 1970s. With the United States and parts of the global banking system essentially insolvent, however, and central banks implementing all manner of unconventional, inflationary policies to try to prop them up, it might be a long time, if ever, before dollar interest rates again provide investors with a positive real rate of return.

When taking all factors into account, the current spot price of gold is probably much too low to provide a sufficient degree of credibility for a restoration of convertibility. It would imply substantial deflationary pressure and threaten the solvency of the banking system with sharply higher interest rates. A somewhat higher price, one that accounts for the interim growth of the money supply, would be more credible.

Adjusting for Growth in the Narrow Money Supply

Although the U.S. money supply has grown dramatically during the four decades of the fiat dollar, much of this growth has occurred since 2008, when the Fed created a huge quantity of dollar reserves to help liquefy the U.S. and global financial system and prevent a systemic meltdown. It has not subsequently drained these reserves and, given that much of the U.S. financial system is essentially insolvent, it is highly unlikely to ever do so. As such, when considering what gold price would be appropriate for a return to conversion today, we need to consider what price would be implied, were the U.S. narrow money supply to be 100 percent backed by gold. Taking the current narrow money supply, defined as bank reserves plus cash

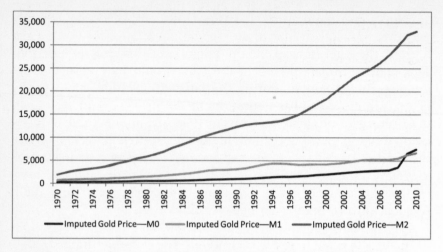

Figure 8.1   Imputed Dollar Gold Prices for Various Measures of the U.S. Money Supply, 100 Percent Backed

Source: Federal Reserve, U.S. Treasury.

in circulation, of about $2 trillion, and dividing this by the official U.S. gold reserve of some 261 billion ounces, yields a current, 100 percent–backed U.S. dollar gold price of about $7,500. (See Figure 8.1.)

Adjusting for Growth in the Broad Money Supply

Today's market gold price is thus at an unreasonably low level when considering at what rate the United States would fix dollar convertibility, were it to move back to a gold standard, because it would probably be highly deflationary and risk a general economic and financial collapse. But even the 100 percent–backed dollar price of $7,500 might not be high enough because even this price does not compensate entirely for the dramatic future money and credit deflation implied by the surge in the broad dollar money supply in recent years.

No one can know exactly when or under what conditions banks might start lending money again and the huge increase in narrow money created by the Fed in recent years would enter general economic circulation, but if it does, there will be a surge in inflation and, naturally, in the price of gold as well. But if the dollar is fixed versus gold, then to the extent that these dollars begin to circulate, this will reduce the implied gold coverage ratio for the broad money supply. And if that ratio should fall sufficiently, it will place upward pressure on interest rates. That will choke off economic growth and place deflationary pressure on the economy.

While this process of money and credit constraint is what a gold standard is all about, we must consider whether this is what U.S. policy makers would want to achieve by a return to a gold standard. If the goal is to retain the U.S. dollar's position as a reserve currency, the convertibility rate is going to have to be credible. Any rate that threatens the solvency of the U.S. financial system will simply not be regarded as credible and thus will fail to restore lasting confidence in the dollar. By implication, it is important to consider what gold price would allow for a substantial portion of the broad money supply to also be backed by gold and to consider what coverage ratios have historically provided general economic and monetary stability.

To allow for previous Fed narrow monetary expansions to actually flow through the economy—that is, through the growth of broad money, thereby facilitating the service of already accumulated debt—the gold price would need to be fixed at a price somewhat higher than the $7,500 per ounce that backs only the narrow money supply. Perhaps much higher. Indeed, the price that might best suit policy makers would be that which implies that the real total economy debt burden declines to a level that can be adequately serviced by the current level of tax revenue.

If the debt burden is seen as too large to be sustainably serviced through current tax revenue, then either the government will have to raise taxes, reducing growth, hurting competitiveness, and potentially leading to an outflow of gold, or alternatively, the government will begin to accumulate additional debt straightaway, leading to a loss of confidence in the ability of the United States to maintain a stable gold exchange rate for the dollar, which would also lead to an outflow of gold. There is no point fixing to gold at all if the rate does not stabilize the U.S. debt level and prevent a large outflow of gold.

Now it is difficult not to get overtly political when talking about marginal tax rates, one of the more popular political footballs to kick around, but there are some simple realities implied by a gold standard. Basically, once you are on it, if you are going to stay on it, you can't print more money than enabled by the real, sustainable growth of your economy. Print too much, and financial markets drain your gold; print too little, and gold reserves swell but at the expense of growth and tax revenues. Given that the U.S. economy is so weak and has been for so long, significantly higher taxes from this point forward are likely to be politically unpopular and, we would argue, damaging for U.S. economic competitiveness. But then higher tax rates are also entirely unnecessary if the dollar convertibility rate is set at a level that makes future debt service manageable at the current level of taxation.

There is good reason, therefore, why politicians might prefer to fix not at today's market price but at a price somewhat higher, for example, one derived from a broad rather than narrow measure of the money supply. For example, let's target a 40 percent coverage ratio for M2. We take 40 percent because this was the original stipulated limit coverage ratio for Federal Reserve notes prior to the Banking Act of 1935. With M2 now approaching $9 trillion, a 40 percent coverage ratio implies a target $13,200 price for gold (Figure 8.2).

Some readers might express disbelief at the prospect of a gold price in excess of $10,000. I would advise these readers to express their disbelief rather at how the Federal Reserve has grown the money supply by such a colossal amount since President Nixon closed the gold window in 1971. All that we have done here is to

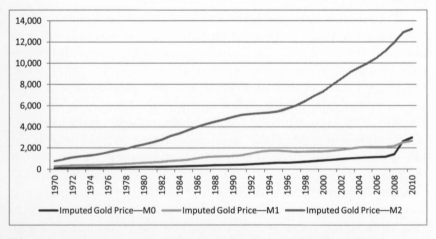

Figure 8.2   Imputed Dollar Gold Prices for Various Measures of the U.S. Money Supply, 40 percent Backed

Source: Federal Reserve, U.S. Treasury.

run the numbers as they are. The alternative to revaluing gold to the levels discussed here is to force an outright contraction of the U.S. broad or possibly even narrow money supply, which would wreak havoc with the banking system and economy, exactly the opposite of what is needed to restore a degree of monetary stability not only to the U.S. economy but also to the global economy.

Having thus explored various ways in which to estimate at what price the United States might reasonably choose to reestablish gold convertibility, we can consider more specifically the actions that would be required to implement this historic change in U.S. monetary policy.

CHAPTER 9

Long-Forgotten Suggestions for How the United States Could Return to Gold

The fiat dollar is 40 years old. Those in favor of a return to a gold standard have never ceased arguing their case. A number of these gold standard advocates have also provided specific recommendations for how to get the United States back onto a gold standard, with minimal disruption to the economy and financial system.

However, the history of the return-to-gold advocates goes back somewhat further. This is because, for some, the Bretton Woods arrangements themselves were flawed. Consider that, under Bretton Woods, the dollar was fixed to gold at $35 per ounce. But actual convertibility was provided only to foreign governments in official transactions with their central banks. Indeed, from 1933, U.S. residents had been forbidden from owning monetary gold by executive order. Although President Franklin D. Roosevelt claimed that this was an emergency measure to help stabilize the failing U.S. banking system in the depths of the Great Depression, the order had never been rescinded. It was only natural that some commentators would wonder why U.S. residents were still forbidden to own gold decades later, when the U.S. economy and financial system were clearly so robust.

One prominent economic commentator of the 1950s and 1960s who argued for a restoration of gold convertibility for U.S. residents was Henry Hazlitt, a columnist for both *Newsweek* and the *New York Times*. In his 1960 book, *What You Should Know about Inflation*, he made the case, now associated primarily with Milton Friedman and the Monetarist Chicago School, that "inflation is always and everywhere a monetary phenomenon." The first chapter of the book, *What Inflation Is*, contains the following:

> Inflation, always and everywhere, is primarily caused by an increase in the supply of money and credit. In fact, inflation *is* the supply of money and credit. . . .
>
> In recent years, however, the term has come to be used in a radically different sense. This is recognized in the second definition given by the American College Dictionary: "A substantial *rise in prices* caused by an undue expansion in paper money or bank credit." Now obviously a rise of price *caused* by an expansion of the money supply is not the same thing as the expansion of the money supply itself. A cause or condition is clearly not identical with one of its consequences. The use of the word "inflation" with these two quite different meanings leads to endless confusion.[1]

Why do you think that Hazlitt went to the trouble in 1960 to write a book about what inflation is? Well, believe it or not, inflation was becoming an issue already in the late 1950s. Hazlitt and others were concerned that inflation, if unchecked, could lead to severe economic consequences. In his view, the most effective way to prevent inflation from becoming a serious problem in the future was to restore domestic gold convertibility. Whereas Bretton Woods allowed for international gold convertibility, U.S. residents and businesses were not permitted to exchange their dollars for gold, at any price.

He was hardly alone in this. Nor was he the first to voice such concerns. In Chapter 9, "Gold Goes with Freedom," he quotes W. Randolph Burgess, former chairman of the executive committee of the National City Bank of New York (today known as Citibank), from a 1949 speech:

> Historically one of the best protections of the value of money against the inroads of political spending was the gold standard— the redemption of money in gold on demand. This put a check-rein on the politician. For inflationary spending led to the loss

---

[1] Hazlitt, *What You Should Know about Inflation* (New York: D. Van Nostrand Company, 1960), Chapter 1.

of gold either by exports or by withdrawals by individuals who distrusted government policies. This was a kind of automatic limit on credit expansion. . . .

There is a group of people today asking for the restoration of the full gold standard immediately in the United States. Today we have a dollar that is convertible into gold for foreign governments and central banks; these people are asking for the same rights to hold gold for our own citizens.[2]

We can see, therefore, that already in the immediate post–World War II period, there were prominent people supporting a restoration of full gold convertibility, primarily because they did not necessarily trust in the sustainability of government or central bank economic and monetary policies.

Yet even back then, these people also understood that restoring convertibility could be disruptive and should be done with care so as not to discredit the very concept of a full gold standard. Hazlitt quotes further from the Burgess speech thus:

> If you try to force the pace by resuming gold payments before the foundations are laid through government policies on the budget, on credit, and on prices, the gold released may simply move out into hoards and become the tool of the speculator.
>
> Gold payments are only part of the building of sound money, and they are in a sense the capstone of the arch.[3]

Hazlitt understood well the nexus where government policies on the economy, generally, and on the gold standard, specifically, meet. As such, while he believed strongly that a return to a full gold standard was highly desirable to check the implementation of unsustainable and economically destructive government policies, it was important to recognize that it is the policies that can be destructive, and thus the policies themselves need to be sorted out. Hazlitt therefore advocated gold convertibility as an important means to an end rather than an end in itself:

---

[2] Hazlitt, *What You Should Know about Inflation* (New York: D. Van Nostrand Company, 1960), Chapter 9.
[3] Ibid.

The gold standard is not important as an isolated gadget but only as an integral part of a while economic system. Just as "managed" paper money goes with a statist and collectivist philosophy, with government "planning," with a coercive economy in which the citizen is always at the mercy of bureaucratic caprice, so the gold standard is an integral part of a free-enterprise economy under which governments respect private property, economize in spending, balance their budgets, keep their promises, and refuse to connive in overexpansion of money or credit. Until our government is prepared to return to this system in its entirety and has given evidence of this intention by its deeds, it is pointless to try to force it to go on a real gold basis. For it would only be off again in a few months. And, as in the past, the gold standard itself, rather than the abuses that destroyed it, would get the popular blame.[4]

Did Alan Greenspan Read Hazlitt?

Alan Greenspan wrote and spoke on economic matters long before he became world famous as chairman of the U.S. Federal Reserve. Indeed, in 1966, he wrote a provocative essay, "Gold and Economic Freedom," in which he echoes rather clearly several of the key arguments put forward by Hazlitt in his various prominent columns and books in the early 1960s. Readers might wish to compare the following quote from Greenspan's essay with the prior quote by Hazlitt:

> Under a gold standard, the amount of credit that an economy can support is determined by the economy's tangible assets, since every credit instrument is ultimately a claim on some tangible asset. But government bonds are not backed by tangible wealth, only by the government's promise to pay out of future tax revenues, and cannot easily be absorbed by the financial markets. A large volume of new government bonds can be sold to the public only at progressively higher interest rates. Thus, government deficit spending under a gold standard is severely limited. The abandonment of the gold standard made it possible for the welfare statists to use the banking system as a means to an unlimited expansion of credit. They have created paper reserves in the form of govern-

[4]Hazlitt, *What You Should Know about Inflation* (New York: D. Van Nostrand Company, 1960), Chapter 14.

ment bonds which—through a complex series of steps—the banks accept in place of tangible assets and treat as if they were an actual deposit, i.e., as the equivalent of what was formerly a deposit of gold. The holder of a government bond or of a bank deposit created by paper reserves believes that he has a valid claim on a real asset. But the fact is that there are now more claims outstanding than real assets. The law of supply and demand is not to be conned. As the supply of money (of claims) increases relative to the supply of tangible assets in the economy, prices must eventually rise. Thus the earnings saved by the productive members of the society lose value in terms of goods. When the economy's books are finally balanced, one finds that this loss in value represents the goods purchased by the government for welfare or other purposes with the money proceeds of the government bonds financed by bank credit expansion.

In the absence of the gold standard, there is no way to protect savings from confiscation through inflation. There is no safe store of value. If there were, the government would have to make its holding illegal, as was done in the case of gold. If everyone decided, for example, to convert all his bank deposits to silver or copper or any other good, and thereafter declined to accept checks as payment for goods, bank deposits would lose their purchasing power and government-created bank credit would be worthless as a claim on goods. The financial policy of the welfare state requires that there be no way for the owners of wealth to protect themselves.

This is the shabby secret of the welfare statists' tirades against gold. Deficit spending is simply a scheme for the confiscation of wealth. Gold stands in the way of this insidious process. It stands as a protector of property rights. If one grasps this, one has no difficulty in understanding the statists' antagonism toward the gold standard.[5]

Even more curious than the possibility that the young Alan Greenspan borrowed heavily from Hazlitt in "Gold and Economic Freedom" is the conundrum of Greenspan's complete transformation from gold convertibility advocate to champion of the fiat dollar. As late as 1981, he was still openly advocating the gold standard. For example, in a *Wall Street Journal* editorial from that year, he wrote about how the United States might go about getting back on gold in gradual fashion:

(Continued)

---

[5] Alan Greenspan, "Gold and Economic Freedom," as featured in Ayn Rand, *Capitalism: The Unknown Ideal,* (New York: Pengiun Group, 1967).

Convertibility can be instituted gradually by, in effect, creating a dual currency with a limited issue of dollars convertible into gold.[6]

It is worth noting that one of Greenspan's early mentors was none other than Ayn Rand, who once quipped that he was "a social climber." He did, indeed, manage to climb all the way to the top of the U.S. Federal Reserve, arguably the most powerful economic policy post in the entire world. But one wonders, to what purpose? Did he ever use his enormous power or influence to try to move the United States back toward a gold standard? If not, why not? Did he simply decide at some point that he was wrong about gold and that the fiat dollar was superior? That unchecked government was better than checked? That welfare statism and associated inflationism was preferable to a free market, sound money economy? Or alternatively, was Greenspan severely disappointed that another one of his mentors, Arthur Burns, failed in his attempts to prevent President Nixon from closing the gold window and that he would continue to try, behind the scenes, to move the United States back toward gold?

The Dr. Jekyll–Mr. Hyde aspect of Greenspan's career has led some to speculate that, perhaps, while at the Fed, Greenspan deliberately and surreptitiously sowed the seeds of the financial crisis of 2008 with easy money and lax banking system regulation. In this way, single-handed and in secret, he undermined the welfare statists' fiat dollar, perhaps fatally, laying the groundwork for a future return to gold. If true, this would be a classic example of truth indeed being far, far stranger than fiction.

Let the Free Market Decide

Hazlitt devotes much space in his book to describing how he believes the United States should go about restoring full gold convertibility. In Chapter 15 of *What You Should Know about Inflation*, "What Price for Gold?" he considers the obvious importance of restoring gold convertibility at a price that will lead to maximum economic and financial stability and, therefore, have the greatest chance of lasting success.

First, he points out how important it is to choose a price that does not lead to a deflationary run into gold that would potentially crash the economy, which, as we have seen, happened with Great Britain following Churchill's decision to restore the pre–World War I gold convertibility rate in 1925:

[6] Alan Greenspan, "Can the U.S. Return to a Gold Standard?" *The Wall Street Journal*, September 1, 1981.

> In periods when public confidence exists in the determination of the monetary managers to maintain the gold standard, as well as in the prudence and wisdom of their policy, gold convertibility may be maintained with a surprisingly low reserve. But when confidence in the wisdom, prudence, and good faith of the monetary managers has been shaken, a gold reserve far above "normal" will be required to maintain convertibility. And today confidence in the wisdom, prudence, and good faith of the world's monetary managers has been all but destroyed.[7]

No doubt Hazlitt would not think particularly highly of the wisdom, prudence, and good faith of today's monetary managers. As such, he would almost certainly recommend erring on the side of restoring convertibility at a much higher gold price than that observed today. This is because, at the current price, the implied gold coverage ratio would be less than ten percent of money supply M2, far lower than what was generally observed back when the United States was officially on a gold standard, yet amid a far, far lower level of monetary credibility.

Given his faith in free markets, it should be no surprise that Hazlitt, while having some idea of what a sensible price for gold convertibility might have been when he wrote his book in 1960, thought that it would be preferable to use the free market to determine an ideal convertibility price before returning to a fully operational gold standard. His specific recommendation is presented in Chapter 19, "How to Return to Gold":

1. The Administration will immediately announce its intention to return to a full gold standard by a series of steps dated in advance. The Federal Reserve Banks and the Treasury will temporarily suspend all sales or purchases of gold, merely holding on to what they have. Simultaneously with this step, a free market in gold will be permitted.

2. After watching this market, and meanwhile preventing any further inflation [i.e., growth in the money supply], the government, within a period of not more than a year, will announce the dollar-gold ratio at which convertibility will take place.

3. On and after Convertibility Day, and for the following six months, any holder of dollars will be entitled to convert them into gold bars, but at a moderate discount on the paper

[7] Hazlitt, *What You Should Know about Inflation* (New York: D. Van Nostrand Company, 1960), Chapter 15.

dollars he turns in. To put the matter the other way, he would be asked to pay a premium on gold bars above the new valuation—equivalent, let us say, to ½ of 1 percent a month. The purpose of this would be to spread out the first demands for conversion and discourage excessive pressure on reserves at the beginning. . . .

4. Six months after Convertibility Day, the country will return to a full gold-bullion standard. Conversion of dollars into gold bars, or vice versa, will be open to all holders without such discounts or premiums and without discrimination.

5. One year later still, the country will return to a full gold-coin standard, by minting gold coins and permitting free conversion.[8]

There you have it. A detailed road map for how the U.S. government, if it desired, could go about restoring a full gold standard in a way that would not cause undue deflationary pressure or threaten the financial system but would, in fact, ensure that, going forward, confidence in the U.S. dollar and U.S. economic policy generally was restored. While there would be nevertheless some economic disruption during the transition, including a wave of inflation as the dollar was devalued sharply versus gold, as discussed earlier, this would be far, far less disruptive than for the United States to wait to be overtaken by events elsewhere.

There is no reason why a future U.S. president must face a sudden dollar crisis far greater than that faced by President Nixon in August 1971. With foresight, U.S. policy makers can make a choice to unilaterally go about restoring gold convertibility. Yes, it will restrict their future freedom of action. But if the dollar suddenly loses reserve currency status, falls sharply in value, and forces up U.S. interest rates, freedom of action will be restricted anyway. Yet in the latter case, this will take place at a time of one or more foreign governments' choosing. U.S. economic officials should ask themselves whether they really want to leave something potentially this disruptive and economically damaging up to foreign governments, some of whom might not be on friendly terms with the United States, or whether they would, in fact, retain greater freedom to act in the future, were they to set about restoring gold convertibility on their own terms sooner rather than later.

[8]Hazlitt, *What You Should Know about Inflation* (New York: D. Van Nostrand Co., 1960), Chapter 19.

The American people also need to ask themselves this important question. In 2011, the deficit arrived on the stage as the crisis issue du jour, with the Republicans in Congress refusing to raise the federal debt ceiling. More recently, criticism of the Federal Reserve has grown, in particular among the current Republican primary candidates. Before long, the dollar itself may be in focus, in particular if it remains in a downtrend.

William Jennings Bryan won the 1896 Democratic presidential nomination with his "Cross of Gold" speech about the dollar and monetary policy. It may be difficult to imagine a U.S. presidential candidate today securing a party nomination or winning an election with a speech about the dollar and about whether the United States should restore the gold standard. But at some point, it is going to happen. The issue will become so immediate, so unavoidable, that a U.S. president will be elected or reelected due largely to whether the candidate supports or opposes a restoration of gold convertibility.

It is my hope that the voters choose wisely.

A Golden Windfall

One of the more obvious, practical investment implications of those who agree with the view that the nominal price of gold is going to rise dramatically as the world moves back to some form of gold standard is to acquire a position in gold as an investment. There are investors, foreign and domestic, who already have had the foresight to invest in gold and other precious metals and dollar hedges and have prospered as the dollar has declined in value. Naturally, these are likely to be relatively wealthy people, but there are many "gold bugs" out there who are not particularly wealthy but, for whatever reason, have long regarded gold as a sensible asset to own to protect against what many have considered an unsustainable path of government finances. So there are no doubt a large number of individuals out there owning a few dozen coins or who have purchased various gold-linked or gold-derivative investments, such as ETFs or gold mining shares, who would all reap a large windfall gain, at least in nominal terms, from a dollar devaluation, or that of fiat currencies generally.

Naturally, these capital gains would be taxable once cashed in, providing the government with a source of tax revenue over time. But the bulk of the gain would remain in the hands of private investors who took a sensible view of their government's limited options for dealing with the debt problem and were proven right by events. It is hard to see why they should not be among the beneficiaries of a return to gold.

10

The Golden BRICs

In the most profound financial change in recent Middle East history, Gulf Arabs are planning—along with China, Russia, Japan and France—to end dollar dealings for oil, moving instead to a basket of currencies including gold.

—Robert Fisk, "The Demise of the Dollar,"
The Independent, October 6, 2009

We have written much about the relative decline of the U.S. economy since the end of World War II and, in particular, since late in the twentieth century. There are, however, two sides to relative shifts, and, in this chapter, we explore the possibility that the larger of the rising global economies, collectively known as the BRICs (Brazil, Russia, India, China), will take the initiative in moving the global economy back onto a gold standard.

The relative growth of the BRIC economies in recent years has been dramatic. As a group, they are already about as large as the U.S. economy and, by extrapolating recent trends, will overtake the United States in the near future (Figure 10.1). They trade increasingly with each other, rather than with the United States. Taken together, these trends imply a growing preference to use each others' currencies in bilateral trade, rather than the dollar. But with no single BRIC economy in a position to dominate the others, it is far more logical for them to move toward the use of an objective reference currency that can be trusted and accepted by all. A gold-backed currency of some sort would be ideally suited for that.

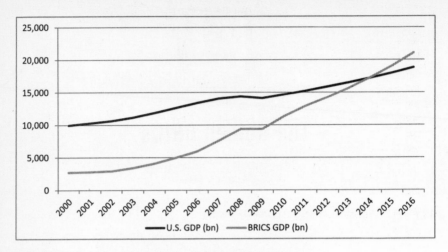

Figure 10.1   The BRIC Economies Are Overtaking the United States
Source: IMF.

As discussed in Part I, the dollar reserve standard is destabilizing the BRIC economies through unwelcome inflation. It also threatens them with huge losses on their accumulated dollar reserve assets at some future point. This helps to explain why the BRICs are already accumulating gold reserves, as well as other real assets such as natural resources. China has been particularly aggressive in this regard, buying up oil and mining companies, acquiring mineral rights, and building real economic infrastructure, such as ports and railways, that facilitate the transport, processing, and manufacture of basic materials into capital and consumer goods. Russia, too, has accumulated a large gold reserve (Figure 10.2). Both countries run large trade surpluses (Figure 10.3), resulting in the unwelcome, indirect importation of inflation from highly expansionary U.S. monetary policies.

The BRICs have also been increasingly assertive in recent years with respect to global monetary arrangements. In the introduction to Part II, we pointed out that in spring 2011 they issued a joint statement that they would prefer for their currencies to be used more widely in global commerce and also to be held more widely as foreign exchange reserves.

Indications that the BRICs and other countries were dissatisfied with the fiat dollar standard go back to the immediate aftermath of

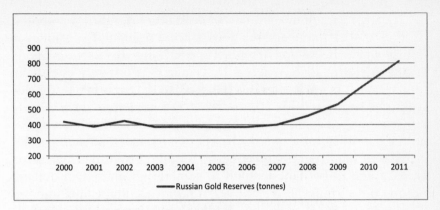

Figure 10.2   Russian Gold Reserves Growing Steadily
Source: IMF, World Gold Council.

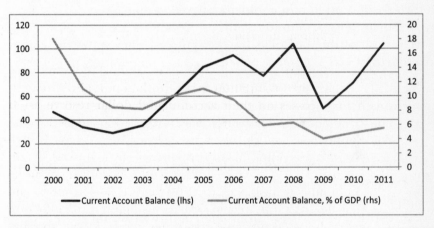

Figure 10.3   Russia's Current Account Surplus Remains Substantial
Source: IMF.

the 2008–2009 credit crisis, when a number of countries explicitly blamed U.S. economic policy for the near-meltdown in the global financial system. In October 2009, veteran journalist Robert Fisk wrote a provocative article, "The Demise of the Dollar," in which he claimed there had been some high-level, behind-the-scenes discussions between the BRICs, oil producers, and a handful of other countries, regarding plans to move away from the dollar as the primary currency for the global oil trade.

If true, this would represent an even more significant potential shift in global monetary relations since President De Gaulle of France made his famous comments attacking the Bretton-Woods arrangements in 1965. Whereas De Gaulle's actions were essentially unilateral—it is unclear to this day to what extent other European countries supported his efforts—what Fisk is describing is a truly international effort to move away from an unhealthy dependence on the fiat dollar and toward a basket of currencies, including gold.

Absent the Bretton-Woods legacy, it would be entirely logical for global trade to be denominated in something other than dollars. Among other things, Fisk observes in his article that China imports 60 percent of its oil from the Middle East. Moreover, China's non-U.S. exports now significantly exceed those to the United States. A similar situation exists with Brazil. That the fiat-dollar should be the transactional currency for such commerce is explained only by historical convention, not contemporary economic logic.

Finally, Fisk also notes that these countries are well aware that, as a result of the fiat-dollar reserve standard, they suffer the consequences of U.S. monetary policies that are increasingly not in their domestic interest:

> America's trading partners have been left to cope with the impact of Washington's control and . . . the hegemony of the dollar as the dominant global reserve currency.[1]

Of course many countries implement monetary policies that are not necessarily appropriate for others. It would be a non-solution to simply replace the fiat dollar with another fiat currency, transferring the "exorbitant privilege" from one country to another.

Even a basket of currencies could be problematic, as all major currencies are currently suffering various forms of economic and financial crises which raise the temptation to inflate away their debts. The Euro-area, the United Kingdom, and Japan all fall into this category. Hence the explicit reference to gold in the article is of particular note. Gold is the only alternative to the dollar which is not at risk of devaluation. From the perspective of the oil-exporting countries, with their vast accumulated wealth and large oil export revenues, transacting in gold, or in an explicitly gold-backed currency, would be most desirable.

[1] Robert Fisk, "The Demise of the Dollar," *The Independent*, October 6, 2009.

Regardless of whether the specifics of this article are true—no official sources have ever confirmed its assertions—it is perfectly plausible to assume that, at a minimum, some of the countries mentioned in the article have considered what to do if, for example, the U.S. Fed continues to print money aggressively or if the United States deliberately chooses to weaken its currency as a matter of policy. By acting in concert, rather than individually, they could probably more effectively deal with the increasing global monetary disruption that such actions would cause. It is thus entirely reasonable to assume that there have been some cross-border discussions on the possibility of coordinated action.

Indeed, there have been other, less provocative but nevertheless pertinent reports in the press during the past year or two regarding cross-border arrangements to reduce dependence on the dollar. Most recently, China and Japan announced that they would begin to rely more on yuan and yen in bilateral trade and less on the dollar.[2] China has also been negotiating with Thailand regarding increasing bilateral trade in their domestic currencies.[3]

In the immediate wake of the 2008-2009 global credit crisis, there were also a handful of such reports. In March 2009, China and Argentina announced a currency swap arrangement.[4] Prior to the Fisk article cited earlier, in July 2009, Reuters reported that Russia, China, and Brazil had prepared to push the idea of a new global currency at the upcoming G8 Summit.[5]

There have also been reports of increased official gold purchases in recent years, an implicit indication that a growing number of countries are seeking to reduce their dependence on dollar reserves. Unlike currency swap and bilateral trade arrangements, the accumulation of gold reserves need not be coordinated. Indeed, a growing preference for gold reserve accumulation could be an indication of a relative lack of global cooperation in monetary affairs. Notwithstanding the various bilateral agreements cited above, these are hardly sufficient to restore the degree of confidence and credibility in global monetary arrangements which prevailed prior to the

---

[2]"China, Japan to Back Direct Trade of Currencies," Bloomberg, December 26 2011.
[3]"China, Government Sign Currency Swap Deal," Bangkok Post, December 23, 2011.
[4]"China, Argentina Reach Agreement on Currency Swap," Bloomberg, March 30, 2009.
[5]"Russia, China to Push Global Currency at G8 summit," Reuters, July 7 2009.

undermining of the U.S. economy and financing system from 2008, and to which this book argues there is no return absent gold.

Let's return briefly to the provocative scenario posed in Chapter 7, in which Russia unilaterally established a new, credible, gold-backed currency. Having been presented with a viable, liquid, gold-backed alternative to the increasingly undesirable U.S. dollar, we assumed that other countries would be quick to adopt the new currency for use in international transactions and as reserves, the most obvious advantage being that this would prevent their economies from being further destabilized by inflationary U.S. monetary policies.

But if the evidence indicates that a number of countries share a common goal of moving away from the fiat dollar toward something more credible, stable, and reliable, why does one of them need to be a first mover? Indeed, as bilateral commercial ties between a number of countries are now greater than those they have with the United States specifically, were a group of countries to move away from the dollar in concert, it would be much less disruptive for any single one of them. Consider also the danger that, if a single country moves first and establishes a gold-backed currency, it might suddenly face huge pressure to revalue as other countries seek to swap a portion of their dollar reserves for the new, gold-backed alternative. That would, of course, hurt relative economic competitiveness.

Recall our previous discussion of the Nash equilibrium: It represents the most desirable collective outcome when each player takes full account of the other players' strategies. As the interests of a single player shift, so must others react, such that the entire equilibrium shifts. Such is the case in the Russia as first-mover example. But what of the present instance, which is, arguably, the opposite, where Russia is, in fact, in good company? What is happening today is that the interests of many players are shifting simultaneously. Only the interests of one major player, the United States, remain essentially unchanged—to inflate the dollar money supply as required to reliquefy its faltering financial system.

As such, it is entirely reasonable to assume that, at some point in the near future, a collection of countries finds a way to move away from the fiat dollar in concert. It would be less disruptive for each and every one of them to do so. The relative impact on economic competitiveness would be substantially less.

In practice, this could be done by following a variation on the hypothetical, unilateral Russian example posed by Rickards. All four BRICs, for example, joined perhaps by Germany and France and some oil-producing countries, could agree to the simultaneous implementation of gold convertibility for their currencies, at a conversion price that would be credible and, hence, sustainable. As is the case in our discussion regarding the United States, the key would be to make certain that, whatever price is chosen, it does not require a deflationary adjustment that would threaten their respective financial systems.

Probably the best way to proceed would be to follow Henry Hazlitt's advice on the matter: Announce your intentions, let markets adjust the relevant exchange rates and their implied gold exchange ratios for a time, and then allow actual convertibility from that point forward. His five-point plan for the United States could be adopted by any number of countries, in concert or individually. The more countries that participated up front, the less overall disruption to global commerce and the sooner the world, having placed gold back at the center of the global financial system, could return to the business of generating sustainable economic growth, rather than continuing to fight the endless series of financial fires associated with the unstable fiat dollar.

Were other countries to take the lead, the United States would quickly find it had no alternative but to go along with whatever gold-backed arrangements this group of countries decided to implement. Gold-backed currencies are simply more credible in a world where trust is lacking. Indeed, if the United States resisted a global move back to gold, it would no doubt find that it faced sharply higher interest rates as a result. Who would prefer to hold unbacked U.S. Treasuries when they could hold gold-backed German, Brazilian, or Chinese government bonds instead?

Sure, the Fed could continue to buy ever-increasing amounts of Treasuries to keep interest rates as low as desired, but then the dollar would not only lose reserve currency status entirely but also become a chronically weak currency, leading to persistent high inflation above and beyond that which would occur were the United States simply to bite the bullet now and restore gold convertibility at a credible rate, as discussed earlier in Part II.

As is well demonstrated by history and as discussed above, rationality does not always prevail in policymaking. There are times when not just one, but a number of countries persist for years in pursing sub-optimal or even seriously damaging economic policies. But that which can't go on, won't, and beyond a certain point, financial markets themselves will force the issue and drag the world, kicking and screaming if necessary, back onto a gold standard. Indeed, in the background of contemporary global economic and financial market developments, there is some evidence that this process is already underway, as we discuss in the next chapter.

CHAPTER

11

When All Else Fails, Enter the Gold Vigilantes

It is, of course, possible that we are giving too much credit to today's economic policy makers. Perhaps there is not a single one prepared to be a first mover back onto gold. Perhaps no consensus can be reached on how to move away from the fiat dollar reserve standard in concert. Perhaps the entire world is going to cling to the inflationary fiat dollar indefinitely, even as this creates ever greater global economic instability. If so, does this imply that the world is not moving back to gold?

Not at all. What it does imply is that the world does move back to gold, just not with any official sanction. *In other words, the world will eventually end up on a de facto gold standard, not a de jure one.*

What do we mean by this? Consider: We have explored how, following a sufficient rise in the price of gold, the excessive, unsustainable debts of today become, in fact, sustainable. The idea that there is too little gold in the world is indeed specious, as Jim Rickards argues. Financial markets can pay whatever they like for gold. Or looked at in the other way, they can *sell* whatever they like for gold. They can sell currencies. They can sell bonds, government or corporate. They can sell stocks. They can sell houses. There is no limit to how much selling can take place as the supply of money, narrow and broad, credit, government and corporate, equities, and property grows. Financial markets can just continue to bid up the price of gold accordingly, to levels that compensate for this ever-increasing supply of everything else.

For those who haven't taken the time to notice, this process is, in fact, already underway. Since 2000, gold has been in a major secular bull market, outperforming currencies, bonds, equities, and property over time, through both the booms and the busts. As our calculations have shown, the gold price is still well below where it needs to be to imply that the overall supply of money and financial assets is not excessively burdensome. But we have already come a long way from the gold bear market that existed through the 1980s and 1990s, years when global productivity growth was quite strong in a historical comparison. Sovereign debt burdens, in particular in the United States, were also far smaller and, it appeared at the time, sustainable. The financial system was better capitalized against potential future losses. The dollar seemed at less risk of falling sharply in value. In sum, there were fewer reasons for investors to protect themselves from excessive debt and leverage by eschewing currencies and financial assets generally and holding gold instead. Into this mix, European central banks were also net sellers of gold accumulated under Bretton Woods decades earlier.

Let us not forget what made the 1980s and 1990s possible: the 1970s. If not for a decade of stagflationary economic deleveraging, culminating in punitive levels of both nominal and real interest rates and the most severe U.S. recession since World War II, a period of U.S. economic renewal would not have been possible. The spectacular rally in gold in the late 1970s thus served an important purpose, helping to place the U.S. economy on a more sustainable path. And it occurred not because of any official policy initiative, but rather because the global financial markets forced the issue through the marketplace itself. (In this regard, it is instructive to note that the rise in the price of gold to over $800/oz in 1980 implied a narrow money M0 coverage ratio in excess of 100 percent.)

Although looked on as a failure of policy—rightly so, we would add—the 1970s experience demonstrates the ultimate supremacy of free markets in the global economy. Sure, governments can distort markets and misallocate resources for a time. The Soviet Union did so for many decades before crumbling amidst soaring inflation as a result. China did much the same, but came to its senses under the hugely underappreciated leadership of Deng Xiaoping in the 1980s, enacting market-based reforms that set the stage for the world's most populous country's spectacular reentry into the global economy. India, the second most populous, flirted with socialism for a time, only to make a similar choice as China eventually. Brazil was arguably just an unusually large banana republic until it got some free-market-based religion in the 1990s. It is no coincidence that, one country at a time, the market wins out over authoritarian, unsustainable policy making.

Now, it is the turn of the United States and Western Europe to learn some harsh lessons, harsher even than those of the 1970s. The United States can do so quickly by acting unilaterally to restore gold convertibility. Another country or group of countries might act first, forcing the issue. Or it might be left to the global financial markets themselves. In any case, gold will play the role it has always played. It will become, either de jure or de facto, the universal, objective reference point for measuring value. Once this has occurred, it will be irrelevant whether a country or group of countries has officially moved back onto a gold standard. The market-pricing mechanism, enabled by reference to gold, will have reasserted itself.

Investors therefore need to prepare. Not only do they need to consider the outlook for the price of gold, or of the implied, sharply reduced purchasing power of paper currencies. They also need to understand what the return to gold implies for interest rate determination, asset valuation and investing generally. It is to this we now turn in Part III.

PART

III

The Economic, Financial, and Investment Implications of the Coming Global Gold Standard

[T]he uncertainty that plagues the investment commitment process is far more pervasive than a decade ago. . . . [T]he most important cause of this uncertainty is inflation, the fear of an increasing rate in the years ahead. An inflationary environment makes calculation of the rate of return on new investment more uncertain.

—Alan Greenspan, "Investment Risk: The New Dimension of Policy," *The Economist*, August 6, 1977

Once the world is back on some form of credible gold standard, the global investment landscape will be completely transformed. Rather than treated as a speculative asset, albeit one with a strong historical track record in providing a store of value, gold will be perceived as the universal, global money, the objective reference point for economic value, relative to which all other values will be determined.

In much the same way that Copernicus placed the sun, rather than the earth, at the center of the universe, thereby simplifying astronomical calculation to the point where Newton was eventually able to explain the movements of both terrestrial and astronomical objects with a single, elegant equation—the law of universal gravitation—placing gold at the center of the global monetary system will greatly simplify economic calculation and asset valuation. By corollary, it will also simplify global commerce and finance generally.

This simplification has a wide range of implications that cut across all aspects of the investment world, in particular, how assets are to be valued vis-à-vis each other and versus gold itself. In Part II, we explored the outlook for the price of gold relative to the dollar and also other currencies, as the world transitions back to some form of gold standard. Regardless of how, exactly, the transition comes about, it is clear that the price of gold, not only in dollar terms but also in terms of any fiat currency, even those regarded as relatively hard, is going to be multiples higher than it is today. Otherwise, the gold standard will simply not be credible because the implied legacy real debt burdens will still dwarf most economies' ability to service that debt. Currencies will collapse anew, and another attempt will be made to return to gold, at an even higher price, until finally a stable equilibrium is reached. From that point forward, financial system rebuilding and sustainable economic growth will be possible.

In this part of the book, we leap forward into the aftermath of the golden revolution that lies in our near future, taking it as a given that some form of stable, credible global gold standard has been established. We then go about applying traditional financial valuation methodologies and metrics to a wide range of assets. While it is difficult to get too precise, there are a handful of general predictions that one can make about things such as:

- The level of interest rates and yields on government bonds.
- Credit spreads for corporate bonds.
- Equity market valuations.
- The level of volatility and options pricing.

Once we have a good feel for how to understand the impact of the coming global gold standard on these topics, we will then be able to consider investment strategy and asset allocation generally. How will investors go about constructing sensible, efficiently diversified portfolios? Where will investors focus when looking for opportunities to outperform? What methodologies or investment styles will be relatively more effective and popular? Each of these questions, and others, will be considered in turn.

This may seem a daunting task. Yet as we shall see, it is not. If there is one thing that a global gold standard will do to the investment landscape, it is that it will greatly simplify it. Returning to our astronomical analogy, Newton's single law and equation of universal gravitation replaced a myriad number of far, far more complex equations, requiring more rigorous and time-consuming calculation, only to arrive at an ultimately incorrect result. Under a global gold standard, investors will find that they have fewer sources of uncertainty with which to deal. As such, they will be able to focus and concentrate on a smaller number of variables and make more sensible investment decisions.

The result is likely to be a far more efficient allocation of capital across companies, industries, and countries around the world, with positive implications for economic growth and financial market stability. This is a good thing for all participants, and the extensive benefits of the future global gold standard—economic, financial, and social—are explored in the conclusion of this book. But now let us get down to the task at hand, put on our investor's hat, roll up our sleeves, pull out our calculator, and see what we can learn about investing under a gold standard. To begin, we will consider how a return to gold will all but eliminate the uncertainty associated with inflation.

The Underestimation and Underappreciation of Uncertainty

Uncertainty is a fact of economic life, for households and corporations, at the micro and the macro level. Yet while some may claim to thrive on uncertainty—entrepreneurs come to mind—what they probably mean is that they enjoy the stimulation that uncertainty provides and the satisfaction that comes from, over time, turning visionary, risky ideas into tangible business plans and, hopefully, success. In this way, success is derived from taking something risky, such as a rather amorphous business idea, and turning it into a practical, cash-generating, going concern, which is far less risky. Entrepreneurs embrace uncertainty and, over time, turn it into something rather more certain, extracting a profit in the process, if and when they succeed.

Economic progress in general can be understood in this way, as moving from rather less to rather more certain conditions. Indeed, as the division of labor and capital underlies all improvements in economic efficiency, with technology an important enabling factor, increasing certainty is critical to sustainable economic growth. Can the mechanic who repairs tractors for a living depend on his farmer customers to grow food, for which he can then exchange his labor at an economically attractive price? If not, there are not going to be any mechanics, and farmers will need to repair their own tractors, implying a loss of farm productivity and lower incomes for all.

Can the miller buy grain, process it into flour, and sell flour to the baker? Can the baker then sell bread to the farmer? What of the transport firm that moves the grain, the flour, and the bread from place to place? Can they depend on the mechanic to repair their vehicles, too? And can they depend on the local gas station to maintain a reliable supply of fuel, oil, and other motor fluids? Can the gas station owner rely on the refiner of those products? Can the refiner rely on the oil transporter to deliver the right grade of oil, to the right refinery, at the right time? Can the transporter rely on the well producer? Can the well producer rely on the drilling equipment provider? Can they both rely on their steel provider, and the steel provider on its iron ore provider? If there is no certainty that labor or goods can be exchanged at a reasonable price both today and in the future, then there can be no specialization, no division of labor, and no economic progress.

When taken in aggregate, the division of labor and capital in a modern economy is so complex that it boggles the mind. It is what economists call a complex system in that it cannot, in fact, possibly be modeled in its entirety or understood by any person or even a group of persons.[1] Yet as stated before, economic progress is impossible without a continuing evolution of the division of labor and capital. Economic progress thus depends primarily on a self-regulating complex system commonly called the free market. The

---

[1]While countless academic papers have been written on the topic of the complex division of labor and capital in the modern global economy, a more poignant treatment of the topic is Leonard Read's famous brief essay, "I, Pencil," which describes in some detail how a pencil is made and, in doing so, illustrates how even an apparently simple economic good is the product of myriad processes. Indeed, as the pencil asserts, "Not a single person on the face of this earth knows how to make me." The entire essay can be found at the Library of Economics and Liberty: http://www.econlib.org/library/Essays/rdPncl1.html

more certainty there exists in this free market, the more economic progress becomes possible.[2]

The role of uncertainty in economic life naturally extends into the world of investing. As with all economic agents, from entrepreneurs to laborers, investors seek to reduce uncertainty over time. They can try to mitigate it, to manage it, to model it, to understand it. But naturally they cannot eliminate it.

There can be no investment without uncertainty. Nor can the price for a given investment be determined without consideration of the risks involved. As the risks grow, with other factors equal, investments become less attractive. More risk equals less investment, and vice versa. This may seem obvious. Yet it is rather easy to overlook that the uncertain value of unbacked fiat currencies and the associated, unsustainable debt burdens so denominated are the single most fundamental investment uncertainty of all. Remove that, and the task of making sensible investment decisions becomes far easier.

Money, Inflation, and Uncertainty

Whether you produce energy, raw materials, manufactured goods, or widgets or provide services such as health care, hairdressing, or dog grooming, to start or expand a business, you are going to need to invest. Funds are going to need to be borrowed, interest paid, and principal repaid. Operating costs and revenues are going to be estimated, and profits will, hopefully, meet or exceed expectations. But under a fiat currency monetary system, each and every one of these estimates—the cost of borrowing, the costs of production, the

---

[2]The reader should note that we are talking about economic progress here, not social. Whether economic progress leads to social progress is a matter of great debate that is beyond the scope of this book. That said, we will offer the following thought: As long as economic progress proceeds in a voluntary fashion, following from choices made free of coercion by the individual members of a society, we consider it at a minimum highly unlikely and most probably impossible for any given set of voluntary economic choices to lead to consistently undesirable social outcomes. Consider this argument in reverse: Should we be confident that involuntary, coerced economic choices would produce superior social outcomes? At the extreme, coerced economic choice is simple slavery. That might produce a desirable social outcome for the masters, but we doubt the slaves would agree.

revenues, the profits—is subject to the uncertainty of inflation. Extrapolated to the global level, where a number of fiat currencies constantly fluctuate, the uncertainty is all the greater.

The greater the uncertainty around inflation, therefore, the greater the investment uncertainty and, other factors equal, the less attractive any given investment will be. As such, one of the first things that we can conclude about a gold standard is that, by restricting money and, by implication, credit growth, a gold standard is going to reduce the negative impact inflation uncertainty has on investment decisions. Other factors equal, less uncertainty equals more, higher-quality investment. Higher-quality investment equals a higher rate of potential economic growth. This is the single most important benefit of a gold standard, one that positively affects an economy at every level.[3] Yet the economic mainstream generally fails to recognize this. We have lived with unstable money and credit growth and the associated economic bubbles and busts for so long that many no longer appreciate the huge benefits that the greater monetary certainty that the future gold standard will provide.

In the following chapters, as we consider how to value various assets under a gold standard, what will most probably strike the reader is not how complicated things are likely to be but rather the opposite. Just as greater monetary certainty will lead to higher-quality investment decisions, it will also greatly simplify all things financial. We begin our discussion at the heart of the modern financial system and the role that central banks are likely to play—or rather not play, as it were—following a return to gold.

---

[3]There are those who believe that economic growth is not necessarily good. They point to things associated with economic growth, such as pollution, for example, that can reduce the quality of life. To deal with such qualitative criticisms of growth is beyond the scope of this book. Let us merely point out that, other factors equal, the *potential* for a higher rate of economic growth cannot possibly be a bad thing; whether a society *chooses* to exercise the potential is another matter, a value judgment. Technology can be put to good or evil uses. But it is fallacious to argue against technology itself.

12

The Role of Central Banking
under a Gold Standard

> No central bank is truly independent. If there is a fundamental
> conflict between the objectives of the government and the
> behavior of the central bank, the central bank, however inde-
> pendent, will sooner or later give in.
> —Milton Friedman, interview published in the
> *Quarterly Journal of Central Banking*, August 2002

It is understandable that the economic mainstream takes central
banking for granted. After all, there is not a single sovereign issuer
of currency today that does not have a central bank.[1] However,
banking is far older than central banking, in the United States and
elsewhere. The U.S. Federal Reserve System came into existence in
1914. Prior to that, there was no single issuer of U.S. banknotes.
Rather, banks issued their own.[2]

---

[1] There are instances in which sovereign nations do not have their own central bank,
such as the members of the euro-area, for example. Also, a handful of countries
use another country's currency. But where countries issue their own national currency, a central bank controls the money supply and normally also regulates banks
and, in some cases, the broader financial system.

[2] The Bank of England, regarded by historians as the model for the Federal Reserve,
opened for business in 1694. However, the oldest central bank still in existence
today is the Swedish Riksbank, dating from 1668.

Recall that in Part I, we took a look at the origins and history of the U.S. dollar, originally defined as a weight of silver or gold. The dollar has subsequently remained the official unit of account of the United States for all domestic commerce, public and private. Yet the dollar was not associated with any paper money printed by a U.S. government institution prior to the Civil War, when greenbacks came into existence as a means of Union war financing. This greenback episode is instructive in considering the role, or rather the relative lack thereof, of a central bank under a gold standard.

A Brief History of the Greenbacks

Wars are expensive, with civil wars exponentially more expensive to prosecute than foreign. Not only must the war be fought but also it must be financed with far fewer domestic resources than would otherwise have been available, were the country in question in one piece, fighting a foreign enemy rather than a domestic foe. Presumably, the opponents in a civil war do not remit taxes or other official revenue to one another, as would be the case in peacetime. And regardless of who wins or loses a given battle, the very act of fighting on domestic soil is likely to cause some degree of destruction to local commerce and, hence, to the available tax base for both sides.

History books on the U.S. Civil War generally make the obvious point that the primary reason the Union eventually won was far superior industrial and other economic resources. The Confederacy had a reasonably well-drilled and well-led army, but time was not on its side. It attempted, in vain, to cause such quick and severe losses on the Union side that the latter would rather settle for peace and recognize separate nations than undergo a potentially prolonged, highly destructive war. As it turns out, the Confederacy underestimated the Union's willingness to completely and sustainably mobilize society for war, under the leadership of President Lincoln. Finally, in 1865, with much of the South in ruins, it was the Confederacy that sued for an essentially unconditional peace, to be followed by years of occupation and reconstruction.

But what the history books tend to overlook as a historical aside is how difficult it was for the relatively prosperous Union to finance the war effort. Not only was the U.S. federal government still tiny at the time, relative to the economy in general, with a correspondingly tiny tax base but also the tax base itself had now shrunk enormously along with the secession of the southern states. Indeed, historians generally agree that the proximate cause of the war was not the underlying moral issue of southern slavery, which had been festering even before the United States formally came into existence in the eighteenth century, but rather the issue of federal tariffs on imports. As southern states generally lacked a manufacturing base, they exported cotton and other raw products to Europe in trade for manufactured products from abroad. As such, the economic burden of the tariffs fell disproportionately on the southern states and were hugely unpopular in the region as a result.

With southern tariff revenue suddenly gone with the outbreak of war, yet huge war mobilization costs to pay, the Union had to find a way to raise additional revenue. This it quickly did by levying an apportioned tax on the northern states. But the amounts generated were far too small to finance the war, even early on. Therefore, the Union set about borrowing the funds instead. One way in which this was done was through the issuance of greenbacks, otherwise known as United States notes.

These notes were denominated in dollars yet bore no interest and could not be redeemed in specie. Naturally, they invariably traded at a discount to actual specie dollar coin or gold-backed U.S. Treasury bonds. This was particularly true early on, as it was unclear how long it would take the Union to successfully prosecute the war, demobilize, and redirect resources toward paying off the accumulated war debt, including an eventual redemption of the greenbacks. There was also the possibility that the Union would simply default on the greenbacks, in particular if the war went particularly badly.

As an example of why greenbacks were regarded as so risky, on December 16, 1861, prior to the issuance of the greenbacks, gold-backed U.S. Treasury bonds plummeted by over 2 percent in a single day, as rumors spread that the United Kingdom planned on entering the war against the Union, something that would have not only lengthened the war in any case but also made it far less of a foregone conclusion that the Union would win. Not long thereafter, the United States suspended specie redemption for outstanding Treasury bonds, forcing banks and investors to roll them over instead. Needless to say, as greenbacks were by design subordinate to gold-redeemable U.S. Treasury notes, their value would have declined by substantially more, had they been trading at the time.

The greenbacks were thus a fiat currency, the first ever issued by the U.S. federal government.[3] Yes, the dollar was still defined in terms of specie at the time, but the greenbacks, although denominated in dollars, were not redeemable. It was only after an unspecified period of time and with a degree of uncertainty and default risk in the potentially long interim that holders of greenbacks could hope that the federal government would eventually buy them back. How, then, did the government get anyone to accept them as a form of payment? Why, by instituting legal tender laws requiring their acceptance. This is but one instructive historical example of how fiat currencies are not willingly held by the public, given a specie-backed alternative.

There were numerous prominent critics of the greenbacks and of the legal tender laws enacted to force their circulation, among them Senator Lovejoy, who said in debate that:

> It is not in the power of this Congress . . . to accomplish an impossibility in making something out of nothing. The piece of paper you stamp as five dollars is not five dollars, and it never will be, unless it is convertible into a five dollar gold piece; and to profess that it is, is simply a delusion and a fallacy.[4]

Proponents of the legal tender laws responded to such criticism in varying ways. Among their arguments was that the supply of greenbacks would be strictly limited, such that confidence in their reliability as a store of value would be high, perhaps even *higher* than gold. As such, they claimed, the poor historical track record of fiat currencies would not be repeated with the greenbacks.

Senator Thomas would have none of it, pointing out, "The experience of mankind . . . shows the danger of entering upon this path; that boundaries are fixed only to be overrun; promises made only to be broken."[5] He was joined by Senator Pomeroy, who was more specific in his predictions:

---

[3] The prefederal Continental Congress did print fiat continentals to help finance the Revolutionary War effort, but those were removed from circulation prior to the establishment of the federal government following the ratification of the Constitution.

[4] Wesley Clair Mitchell, *A History of the Greenbacks* (Chicago: University of Chicago Press, 1903), 56.

[5] Wesley Clair Mitchell, *A History of the Greenbacks* (Chicago: University of Chicago Press, 1903), 57.

The same necessity which now requires the amount of inconvertible paper now authorized, will require sixty days hence a similar issue, and then another, each one requiring a larger nominal amount to represent the same intrinsic value.[6]

Proponents also tried a completely different tack, which was to build confidence in the greenbacks by making them convertible into gold-backed U.S. Treasury bonds, for which redemption in specie had already been suspended:

> Section one of the bill provided that holders of legal-tender notes could at any time exchange them at par for 6 percent twenty-year bonds. Under this arrangement, it was supposed, the value of the [Greenbacks] could never be less than that of the bonds, and, as bonds could by law not be sold for less than par, it followed that the notes could not greatly depreciate. Unfortunately for the argument, even while Congress was debating the bill, bonds were selling in New York at 90 cents upon the dollar. . . .[7]

This line of argument was thus self-defeating, as the entire point of the legal tender laws was to prevent government-issued fiat money from trading at a discount in the first place. If even gold-backed Treasury bonds could trade at a discount—presumably because investors discounted the risk that redemption might be suspended indefinitely—then so could the non-interest-bearing, irredeemable greenbacks.

Proponents thus found themselves in a corner. If it were possible for the greenbacks to trade at a discount to coin specie, then:

> [C]oin would disappear from circulation . . . prices would rise suddenly, fixed incomes would decline, creditors be defrauded, and the widows and orphans would suffer. Senator Collamer showed how depositors in savings banks would lose by depreciation, and Senator Fessenden how labor would be injured by a rise of prices exceeding the rise of wages. Finally, Mr. Crisfield

---

[6]Wesley Clair Mitchell, *A History of the Greenbacks* (Chicago: University of Chicago Press, 1903), 58.
[7]Ibid.

represented forcibly the instability of a paper standard of value
and the consequent danger to business. . . .[8]

And finally:

the resort to an irredeemable paper currency was a practical
confession of bankruptcy, and would therefore injure the credit
of the government, and make less favorable the conditions on
which it could borrow . . . the government might as well lose 25
percent on the sale of her [sic] bonds, as to be obliged, in avoiding it, to pay 25 percent more for everything she buys.[9]

In the end, amid the backdrop of war, the greenback proponents
carried the day. The key argument on which they always fell back
was that the war made the hitherto repugnant (and arguably uncon-
stitutional) idea of a fiat currency tolerable as a limited, temporary,
necessary, emergency measure. Little did they know that, a little over
a century hence, an irredeemable fiat dollar would be regarded as
just the normal state of affairs.

Why Fiat Currencies Require Legal Tender Laws and Central Banks (and, by Implication, Why a Gold Standard Does Not)

The greenback debate helps to illustrate just how a fiat currency is
differentiated from a specie-backed one and, by implication, how a
central bank is naturally more associated with the former.

The most obvious point is that a fiat currency cannot compete
with specie absent legal tender laws. Other factors equal, claims on
specie will always be in greater demand than irredeemable notes.
Thus there must be a central authority that can enforce the acceptance of unbacked fiat notes, or they will collapse in value and be
replaced by specie, as per Gresham's Law.

A fiat currency also requires a central authority as issuer, for two
reasons. First, unlike specie coin, which is ultimately a standardized
measure of weight not necessarily requiring legal recognition, a fiat
currency is not going to be accepted for payment unless it is unam-

[8]Wesley Clair Mitchell, *A History of the Greenbacks* (Chicago: University of Chicago
Press, 1903), 59.
[9]Ibid.

biguously genuine legal tender, with a high degree of confidence that it is not simply manufactured counterfeit.

Second, to manage supply, there must be a single authority behind a fiat legal tender. If multiple entities are entitled to issue the same currency, then naturally, each has an incentive to print as much of it into existence as possible, making it impossible to control supply and, by implication, prices.

There is then the issue of interest. The greenbacks were non-interest-bearing and intended to serve as a legal tender currency. However, the debate in Congress made clear that, as fiat currency, they were likely to trade at a discount to specie or specie-backed bonds. Something that trades at a discount to face value has an imputed interest rate, which is a function of the size of the discount and the term to maturity.

This brings us to the following: Although this was not the case with the greenbacks, in the event that banks are required to accept the legal tender at face value to specie, then they will not be able to earn interest on fiat reserves and will hold as little of it as possible. Specie will be driven out of circulation into private, nonbanking hoards. As this would weaken the banking system, there arises the issue as to whether the government or other authority should set minimum reserve requirements to prevent banks from operating with dangerously low capital ratios.

Now in theory, the government itself, rather than an authorized agency thereof, can be the issuer of a fiat currency. Indeed, this was the case with the greenbacks. The government can also manage the money supply and, of course, can function as the regulatory agent, including setting reserve requirements. But notice that all of these functions, none of which is required under specie standard, are typically given over to a central bank in practice. The simplest explanations are historical ones. Banks were, naturally, the first issuers of banknotes, although these were originally always backed by specie of some kind. As such, it naturally followed that, when banknote issuance was placed under a single authority, a designated bank would take the role.

Also, central banking predates the general introduction of fiat currencies. Their origin lies in the need of various European crowns to finance wars or other spending. Monarchs and parliaments had varying degrees of taxing authority yet, by the seventeenth century, found they were increasingly reliant on bank borrowing. By creating a central bank implicitly backed by the sovereign taxing authority, it was assumed that borrowing costs would be lower than otherwise, as sovereigns would in effect be borrowing against their future tax revenues rather than in unsecured fashion through private banking middlemen who would require a higher rate of interest.

As seen in the greenback debate, this was a key argument of the proponents for legal tender laws. As such, both fiat currencies and central banking have their origin in sovereign financing rather than in banking generally, which grew out of private commerce, using specie as a market-based medium of exchange. To the extent that there were legal tender laws, in practice these were enacted to regulate the value of the coin of the realm and to provide the crown with seigniorage income, as new coinage was introduced via sovereign mining operations, domestically or via colonies such as those of the New World.

Not incidentally, the opponents' views on how the greenbacks and legal-tender laws would distort the Union's financial system and economy were eventually vindicated by events. Not only were multiple series of greenbacks issued in the following years but also the negative impact on commerce was palpable:

> [S]uspension of specie payments threw the monetary circulation of the loyal states into disorder by causing the withdrawal of gold and silver coin from common use as money. . . .
>
> [T]hough the inconveniences caused by these changes in the medium of exchange were not slight, they were less serious than were the results produced by the change in the standard of value. . . . The legal tender acts substituted the greenback for the gold dollar as this unit. Now the gold dollar had contained 23.2 grains of pure metal, but the greenback dollar that took its place was at no time during the war worth so much as this. A year after the passage of the first legal-tender act a greenback dollar would purchase by 14.5 grains of gold. . . .
>
> It was this depreciation of the money unit that gave rise to the most complicated and interesting economic developments of the war period. Of course, in exchanging commodities for money men were unwilling to give as much for a dollar worth 9 grains of gold as they had given for the dollar worth 23.2 grains. What is tantamount to giving less goods for the dollar, they demanded more dollars for the goods. The decline in the

specie value of the greenbacks, therefore, produced an extraordinary rise of prices. . . .[10]

That the forced introduction of an unredeemable fiat currency into circulation would lead to a surge in price inflation is hardly surprising. As Henry Hazlitt and Milton Friedman reminded us in the 1960s, inflation is always and everywhere a monetary phenomenon.

The greenback episode also demonstrates that, notwithstanding the monetary aspect of price inflation, it is, in fact, ultimately a political phenomenon. Absent politicians' willingness to override markets' monetary preferences, thereby driving gold and silver out of circulation, inflation would be a nonissue. In this regard, the historical legacy of the greenback episode, associated with what was, ultimately, a triumphant if horribly costly Union victory in the war, led to a more open mind at the federal government level regarding the idea of a fiat dollar and the associated inflation. As we know, in 1971, the United States embarked on another fiat currency misadventure, yet to conclude.

Free Banking: Why Central Banking Is Optional under a Gold Standard

It should now be clearer why central banking is in theory entirely unnecessary under a gold standard but necessary under a fiat one. First, there need be no single issuing authority. Recall that according to the Coinage Act of 1792, the U.S. dollar originally referred to the Spanish milled dollar or piece of eight rather than to anything issued by the Continental Congress or the federal government that succeeded it. Second, as the supply of specie cannot be arbitrarily inflated, there need not be a central authority to control the supply.

Third, whereas banks are not inclined to hold non-interest-bearing, nonspecie reserves, they have a clear incentive to hold gold and silver. Hold too few reserves, and depositors will be reluctant to place money with the bank unless rates of interest on deposits rise. The higher the rate paid on deposits, the less profitable the bank. As such, on a gold standard, market forces can be expected to

[10]Wesley Clair Mitchell, *A History of the Greenbacks* (Chicago: University of Chicago Press, 1903), 142.

prevent banks from holding dangerously low levels of reserves. Those that do will find that they are driven out of businesses or taken over by their more sensible competitors.

This brings us to the concept of free banking. It should come as no surprise that many advocates of returning to a gold standard also advocate a form of what is generally referred to as free banking, in which banks operate in an essentially free market, more akin to how, under capitalist systems, most normal industries tend to operate.[11]

Nonfinancial corporations tend to decide for themselves, for example, what products they would like to manufacture or what services they want to provide, using which materials or human resources, priced at what price, in which market, and so forth. Those that choose to manufacture products or provide services that customers actually want, at prices they can reasonably afford, and market these effectively tend to make a profit. Those that don't either change what they are doing or are ultimately forced into bankruptcy and reorganization, freeing up their assets for use in some other, presumably more profitable enterprise.

As we have seen in our discussion of the greenbacks and the nature of fiat currency and legal tender laws, the fact that the world is currently on a fiat dollar standard effectively requires banking to be a highly regulated industry. Yes, there is a degree of competition and freedom of action at the margin, but the vast bulk of what banks do is determined by a set of rules laid down by the central bank or other regulatory authority:

- Banking licenses are normally expensive and time-consuming to obtain, stifling competition and favoring those with political connections.
- Banks are required to use the legal-tender currency issued by the central bank.
- Banks must maintain a mandated portion of reserves.
- Banks' cost of funding is determined by the central bank, normally in the form of a security repurchase or repo rate, or

---

[11]Among prominent modern advocates of free banking are Lawrence White and George Selgin. Nobel laureate Friedrich Hayek also supported free banking.

that for borrowing reserves (i.e., covering a temporary short-fall) from the central bank.

- Banks' lending activities tend to be restricted in various ways or, alternatively, subsidized to benefit defined groups.
- Banks can be summarily suspended or even shut down if they are found to be noncompliant with any given regulation.

Central banking can certainly coexist with a gold standard. The era referred to as the classical gold standard period, 1880 to 1914, began and concluded with European central banks in operation at each step of the way. The point, however, is that under a gold standard, the role of central banks is considerably circumscribed. Nowhere is this more likely to be the case than with setting the level of interest rates, something that is taken for granted under a fiat regime but, under a gold standard, is necessarily left largely to the free market, as we shall see. A simple way to illustrate this is to discuss how a so-called currency board functions.

How to Disarm a Central Bank

As discussed before, we take it for granted that central banks, as part of their remit, set short-term interest rates and control the money supply. While this is indeed common, there are exceptions where the central bank leaves interest rates and the money supply to the market to determine. A simple example of this in practice is that of a currency board, such as that operating in Argentina in the years 1991 to 2002. This is when a country, normally with the central bank acting as agent, decides to peg its currency to that of another, normally much larger, country.

As a first step in establishing a currency board, a central bank accumulates some amount of reserves of the foreign currency that is to serve as the peg. The central bank then maintains this peg by allowing the domestic level of interest rates to rise in the event that the foreign exchange markets prefer to sell the domestic currency and, conversely, allow the domestic level of interest rates to fall in the event that the markets prefer to buy. The accumulated reserves are to provide temporary liquidity for these transactions only. The point of the policy is not to accumulate reserves; rather, it is to maintain a stable exchange rate. That said, the country does earn interest on the reserves, a form of seigniorage income comparable to charging a premium for newly issued coins of the realm or—perhaps a better comparison if the currency is pegged to an inflating currency—clipping coins as they pass through the Treasury.

In practice, the result is that the country operating a currency board in effect outsources its monetary policy to the issuer of the reference currency. This is because the foreign exchange markets will perceive an essentially risk-free arbitrage opportunity in the event that a credible currency board rate of interest is materially above or below that of the reference currency. As such, they will buy or sell currency in whatever amount is required until the interest rates either converge or, more likely, narrow to a level that represents a small risk or liquidity premium for holding the pegged currency, but nothing more.

The observed risk premium in this case becomes a market-determined barometer of the sustainability of the currency board country's domestic fiscal and other, nonmonetary economic policies, with monetary policy outsourced. This can be a highly useful arrangement for a government seeking to implement painful economic reforms, for example, reducing government expenditures and getting wage inflation under control. Indeed, these are precisely the reasons why Argentina chose to adopt a currency board in 1991, with the peso pegged to the U.S. dollar.

As we have seen, the role of central banks will be highly circumscribed under a gold standard. In particular, central banks may continue to set interest rates at the margin, but they will have a severely limited ability to set rates far from where the market would place them for any sustained period of time. As such, we now turn to how interest rates, the fundamental building block of all finance, will be determined by the financial markets under the future gold standard.

CHAPTER 13

Valuation Fundamentals under a Gold Standard

The [true rate of interest] is essentially independent of the supply of money and money-substitutes, notwithstanding the fact that changes in the supply of money and money-substitutes can indirectly affect its height. But the market rate of interest can be affected by changes in the money [supply].
—Ludwig von Mises, *Human Action*, Chapter 19, Section 6

Financial assets are legal claims on future cash flows of varying degrees of certainty. As such, any methodology for valuing assets must contain an assumption for the time value of money, or interest, as well as a way for dealing with the uncertainty necessarily associated with anything that lies in the future. In this chapter, we begin with a consideration of these fundamental concepts and subsequently apply them to a range of assets.

Savings, Investment, Consumption, and Time Preference

Let us return briefly to the topic of economic uncertainty, introduced earlier, from the perspective of an investor. Investors always have a choice of either saving or investing. As uncertainty decreases, other factors equal, investors are willing to invest more, and vice versa. Yet what one investor saves remains available, via the banking and financial system, for others to invest. As such, we recognize one of the fundamental accounting identities of economics, that savings must equal investment:

$$\text{Savings (S)} = \text{Investment (I)}^{1}$$

As investment opportunities become more attractive and investors thus want to invest relatively more and save relatively less, the rate of interest on (or price of) savings must necessarily rise, such that savings and investment remain in balance. Alternatively, in the event that investment becomes relatively less attractive for some reason and investors become more inclined to save, then the rate of interest will decline.

Economists refer to this phenomenon as time preference, which also applies to consumption. At any given point in time, a household can either save or consume. What is saved today is consumed in the future, reflecting a preference to do so. As the propensity to consume today increases, households save relatively less, and, to keep savings and investment in balance, the rate of interest on savings must rise. Alternatively, if households become more inclined to save today and consume more in future, then the rate of interest will decline accordingly. Looking at the bigger picture, what one household saves out of their income becomes available for investment. As such, we recognize another macroeconomic accounting identity, that income, minus savings (or investment), must equal consumption:

$$\text{Income (I)} - \text{Savings (S)} = \text{Consumption (C)}$$

Interest rates are thus properly understood as the prices that keep these identities between income, savings/investment, and consumption in balance.

---

[1] For simplicity, by investment we mean net investment, that is, net of depreciation. All productive assets depreciate over time to some degree. As such, the greater the capital stock in relation to the economy generally, the more that will need to be saved to maintain it over time. This is the simplest way to understand why an economy can save/invest too much: It ends up with a capital stock that depreciates at a greater rate than what it produces can be consumed, implying a net economic loss. Ideally, a capital stock will grow only to the point that what it produces is fully consumed, no production is wasted, and there is no excessive depreciation. For more on this topic, see Robert Solow's growth model, presented in "A Contribution to the Theory of Economic Growth," *Quarterly Journal of Economics* 70, no. 1 (1956), 65–94.

The Concept of the Risk-Free Interest Rate

Economists use the concept of a risk-free interest rate to separate the concept of the time-value of money from that of credit risk. If one person lends money to another, naturally, they expect to get it back. If they perceive zero risk that they will not get it back, then the interest rate charged is risk-free in that there is no default risk included in the calculation.

This is different from saying that there is no interest rate risk, which increases with maturity. For example, if a bank lends money to a business over a 10-year period at a 2 percent risk-free rate, but then, for whatever reason, time preferences change in favor of current investment/consumption over future and the going 10-year interest rate rises to 4 percent, then, if the loan is marked to market, it will have fallen in value, as it earns only 2 percent rather than the market rate of 4 percent.

This price risk associated with changes in the market level of interest rates is not credit or default risk but pure interest rate risk, and it explains, for example, why default risk-free government bond prices are nevertheless volatile and move inversely to yields. In the financial jargon, interest rate risk is divided up into *duration*, which for non-coupon-paying instruments increases linearly with maturity, and *convexity*, which increases exponentially.

Real versus Nominal Interest Rates in Theory

When discussing interest rates, it is important to distinguish between real and nominal, the difference between the two being inflation. Recall that savings equals investment. But if over any given time period, the amount of real savings is diluted by the creation of new money, then, other factors being equal, the real rate of interest will be lower. And in the event that the money supply shrinks during any particular time period, the real rate of interest will be higher. As real rates are those that represent the real time value of money, they are the ones that keep real incomes, savings/investment, and consumption in balance.

Whether nominal interest rates rise and fall with inflation depends on whether such inflation is seen or unseen. If financial markets perceive correctly that inflation is rising, then nominal rates will rise accordingly, and vice versa. In practice, this is not always the case. If, for example, financial markets fail to perceive that inflation is rising (i.e., the money supply is growing), the result will be an investment and/or consumption boom that must, by definition, eventually turn into a bust. This is because, over time, real incomes, savings/investment, and consumption must be in balance, as per the accounting identities introduced earlier.

A Primer On Rational Expectations Theory (RET)

The 1970s was the decade of the dreaded stagflation, something that traditional Keynesian economic models implied could not happen. This is because, within a traditional Keynesian framework, there is a stable relationship between inflation and unemployment known as Okun's law (after economist Arthur Okun). As inflation rises, unemployment declines, and vice versa. This implicitly assumes, however, that nominal interest rates do not respond to inflation ex ante but rather only ex post. Originally posed by economist John Muth, RET was used by other prominent economists, such Milton Friedman and Robert Lucas, to ridicule this assumption as grossly naïve. Financial markets may not be perfect but they are, according to RET, rational enough to discount macroeconomic policies that have traditionally proven to be inflationary. As such, nominal interest rates rise and fall along with inflation expectations, preventing an artificial decline or increase in real rates (via inflation or deflation) from translating into an actual investment boom/bust. The stagflationary 1970s were to an extent predicted by RET and, in retrospect, rather well explained by it. The persistent weakness of the economy amid generally rising inflation from the mid-1970s through early 1980s is thus better explained by structural factors (e.g., that the United States was not energy efficient enough to absorb higher oil prices and had also become relatively less competitive internationally in a number of key industries, such as car manufacturing), and RET postulates further that the stagflation thus ended not only because policy makers decisively reversed inflationary policies via sharply higher interest rates and lower money supply growth in the early 1980s but also because the U.S. economy made some important structural adjustments by the mid-1980s, including becoming generally more energy efficient, and also benefited from increased global trade, in particular with the Pacific Rim, which had become considerably more affluent.

Incidentally, the Nobel Prize in Economics was recently awarded to three economists for their work on RET, including Muth, as mentioned earlier.

Real versus Nominal Interest Rates in Practice

Under a fiat currency standard, with legal tender laws enforcing its use and central banks setting interest rates, there is no free market in money. Interest rates are not set by a reconciliation of supply and demand for savings; rather, they are set by a central bank in an attempt to achieve certain policy goals, such as meeting a target rate of growth in a consumer price index. By altering the growth rate of the money supply and arbitrarily setting short-term or even long-term interest rates, they seek to manage economic activity to some end, the most common ostensible reason being to maintain economic stability. But with few exceptions, the history of central banking is not, as we have seen, a history of maintaining stability at all or even of providing greater stability to the financial system specifically. Rather, as demonstrated in Part I, it is a history of fuelling an ongoing series of bubbles and busts, stepping in where necessary to save the financial system from itself. As this process has critically undermined the current, dollar-centric, global monetary order, a return to a gold standard has become necessary and inevitable.

Fortunately, once under a gold standard, in which material monetary inflation becomes essentially impossible absent a formal exit or devaluation from that standard, then nominal interest rates are going to fall in line with real. Moreover, it will be impossible for central banks, assuming that they still exist, to hold interest rates at levels other than where a free market in money would place them and still remain on a gold standard. To the extent that they do diverge, they will be an indication that financial markets are concerned that macroeconomic policies are incompatible with adherence to the gold standard, that governments are behaving recklessly, and that there is a growing risk of a currency devaluation or departure from the gold standard at some point in future. Governments, in other words, will find poor policies more difficult to hide and, therefore, more difficult to implement in the first place.

To some extent, this is what is being observed in the euro area today. Euro-area governments no longer control their printing presses. Of these, several have followed expansionary, even reckless fiscal policies in recent years and have accumulated clearly unserviceable debt burdens. However, rather than seeing their currencies depreciate as a consequence of poor policies, they find their borrowing costs are rising. This increase in interest rates is not a function of current inflation, which is contained by the generally pragmatic monetary policies of the European Central Bank (ECB); rather, it reflects the growing risk that these countries will, in the near future, either default on these debts, exit the euro area and devalue their currencies, or some combination of the two.

The euro area, in this respect, thus functions as a kind of quasi gold standard, imposing market-based interest rate discipline on governments that run unsustainable policies. At the time of writing, Greece is already restructuring its colossal accumulated debt. Portugal and Ireland are likely to do the same over the coming year. It is also probable that, at some point in future, both Spain and Italy will require a debt restructuring. The alternative for these countries would be to leave the euro area, akin to withdrawing from a gold standard. Without the credible backing of the ECB however, withdrawal will naturally lead to a dramatic currency depreciation, destroying much of the accumulated paper wealth of the country in question. Hyperinflation and a complete collapse of the new domestic currency are entirely possible. The Greeks and others are no doubt aware of this risk, hence their extreme reluctance to ditch the euro and introduce a neodrachma or other national currencies instead.

Much the same discipline imposed by membership in the euro area would be observed under an actual gold standard. In fact, it would be even stricter. This is because although the ECB, as a supranational central bank, cannot set monetary policy for just one or two member countries in debt trouble, nevertheless, there is the possibility that such countries might be bailed out by other members. Also, as we have seen over the course of the past year, the ECB has the flexibility to provide temporary emergency financing to members, something that it has been doing with the express intent of buying time so that some sort of comprehensive bailout of weak euro-area sovereign borrowers can be arranged.

Gold, as a nonprintable, finite substance, cannot simply be conjured into existence as desired to provide a temporary source of confidence in a failing financial institution, sovereign or other public entity—or any borrower for that matter. Under a gold standard, financial support, absent a windfall acquisition of additional gold, comes with an immediate, objective cost: an incrementally higher rate of interest. The more one borrows relative to one's ability to service the debt, the higher the interest rate demanded by the financial markets.

Such discipline, in practice, essentially guarantees that attempts by fiscal or monetary authorities to implement clearly unsustainable policies will nearly simultaneously not only be exposed as such but also, as such exposure occurs through the interest rate itself, quickly become prohibitively costly such that they are likely to be abandoned unless other commitments are scaled back accordingly. Under a gold standard, the fiscal authorities will be able to increase spending on only programs that represent the most important priorities, something that, one could argue, is highly likely to result in a sensible rationalization of economic policy generally.

Estimating the Level of Interest Rates

As we have seen, absent unsustainable macroeconomic policies, under a credible gold standard, interest rates will be determined by the underlying real supply and demand for funds, both functions of economic time preference. But then what is the interest rate likely to be?

Recall that by placing gold at the center of the economic and financial universe, calculation is greatly simplified. In this case, the interest rate will reflect nothing more than the real time value of money; it will be a direct, undistorted expression of time preference on the part of investors and households. As savings preferences rise, so will the interest rate. If investment and consumption preferences rise instead, so will the interest rate. As always, the interest rate will be at the level that maintains our macroeconomic accounting identities:

$$\text{Savings} = \text{Investment}$$

and

$$\text{Income} - \text{Savings}/\text{Investment} = \text{Consumption}$$

Therefore, the real time value of money should be a function of the sustainable potential growth rate of the economy. If, as is sometimes assumed, a developed industrial economy can grow sustainably at around 3 percent per annum, then this would probably give an

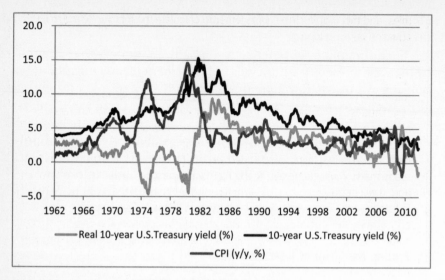

Figure 13.1   Ten-Year U.S. Real Interest Rates through the Decades
Source: Federal Reserve.

indication of the rough magnitude of the long-term risk-free interest rate under a gold standard. For an economy capable of growing sustainably at a higher rate, the rate would be higher, and vice versa. In Figure 13.1, we see that 10-year U.S. real interest rates have tended to fluctuate around a level more or less in line with that of trend GDP growth, notwithstanding much cyclical volatility from time to time.

Why GDP Is a Poor Measure of Economic Growth in a Modern Economy

Gross domestic product (GDP) is the most common measure of total economic income used by the economic mainstream today. Unfortunately, it is a highly flawed measure, better designed to measure the available tax base rather than the real economy. It also obscures the quality and sustainability of growth.

The GDP is based on the economic identity that total economic income must equal total economic production. It is then calculated by dividing production up into various sectors, most commonly into private-sector consumption (C), investment (I), government spending (G), and net exports to other economies, and then adding them all together to calculate the total. So a typical GDP equation is the following:

$$GDP = C + I + G + (E - I),$$

with imports (I) subtracted from exports (E) to calculate net exports.

Thus GDP estimates the total value of all economic transactions during any given period. It does not measure activity for which no transaction takes place. So, for example, if you purchase food at a supermarket but prepare the meal at home, the latter value added will not be captured in GDP. Purchase a ready-made meal, however, requiring no preparation, and the entire value added will be captured by GDP. Whereas the purchase of the ready-made meal is taxable, the final preparation of a home meal is not. As such, GDP captures only visible, not invisible, activity. But consider: Is preparing a meal at home somehow less valuable or less desirable than purchasing a ready-made meal? For a household that can get by on one income, regular home meal preparation might be considered a nice luxury, whereas for a family that requires two incomes, the regular purchase of ready-made meals might be seen as an unfortunate necessity of their less affluent financial position.

The GDP also treats all transactions equally, adding them to each other even in the event that they basically cancel each other out. For example, let's say two businesses sue each other over some dispute. On both sides, they pay out substantial legal fees. Perhaps they settle their dispute in the end with neither side benefiting. Yet the legal fees on both sides are added to GDP. Measured in this way, a general increase in litigation would be perceived as economic growth comparable, say, to building new factories and homes. It is highly dubious to assume, however, that society would regard both types of GDP growth as comparable or desirable.

Also, as far as GDP is concerned, there is no difference between growth in private consumption and investment and that of the government. Yet the latter cannot add to growth at all without first taking income away from the private sector, as all government income originates as taxation. (To the extent that the government finances itself through debt issuance, this is a claim on future taxation.) When the government sector is small, so is this distortion. But as a government sector grows relative to the real economy, it becomes significant. What GDP calculates as economic growth could be just a growing transfer of income from the private sector to the government via taxation.

This is the main reason that the neo-Keynesian economic mainstream is always quick to point out that cuts in government spending will depress GDP growth, at least temporarily. But when they fail to see is that, while GDP may indeed decline as a result, overall, real economic activity may not, in particular when the less visible is included. Referring back to our example, if there were

(Continued)

less government spending and thus less taxation, some two-income households might find they can, in fact, get by on one income. As such, one member would be available at home to provide child care and meal preparation. Yes, this would reduce GDP, but would it improve, or worsen, this household's economic position? The question answers itself and demonstrates this major flaw in GDP.

Another shortcoming with GDP is that as economic transactions necessarily take place in nominal values, nominal GDP grows with inflation as well as with the real economy, which grows only in volumes of goods and services. As such, real GDP is derived from nominal values by using a price deflator, which attempts to measure by how much all the various goods and services have risen in price over the same time period.

Although measures of price changes, ranging from consumer price indices (CPI) to GDP deflators, are taken for granted as definitive measures, in practice they are just estimates, subject to various kinds of measurement error. It should be no surprise, for example, that the United States has changed the way it calculates both the CPI and the GDP deflator through the years. If either of these were clearly so definitive, they would not be works in progress.

Lest the reader think that such changes are not material, it is rather eye-opening to learn that the way the CPI is calculated, for example, has changed so much in recent decades that, were the old methodology still in use, it would show CPI currently running at a level as high as during the second half of the 1970s, the years of the dreaded stagflation. Yet the U.S. Federal Reserve, pointing toward the low level of the CPI today, claims it is still concerned primarily by deflation rather than inflation!

It should be clear that, given these various flaws in the GDP methodology, it gives an incomplete and potentially highly misleading picture of an economy, in particular whether the growth taking place is real, healthy, or sustainable. Its widespread use largely reflects the historical legacy of its introduction at a time when economies were primarily production rather than service based, when the government sector was far smaller, and when inflation was much lower, in large part because countries were on a gold standard. As such, it was much more suitable back then than today.

Estimating the Term Structure of Interest Rates

As is the case under a fiat standard, under a gold standard, short-term rates would normally be considerably more volatile than long-term rates. These fluctuations, however, would not reflect changes in inflation or inflation expectations as they would be so stable as to be immaterial. They would, therefore, reflect the dynamism of the real economy, that is, the real demand for and supply of savings.

As we are talking about real rates of growth and real rates on savings, there is no inflation calculation to worry about, no potential material loss of purchasing power that must be incorporated into the rate as an inflation risk premium, something that is normally included in interest rate modeling assumptions.

A traditional model for interest rates normally contains the following components:

- An assumption for the future path of policy rates.
- A risk or term premium to compensate investors for uncertainty, which tends to be higher at longer than at shorter maturities.

However, as we have seen, under a gold standard, interest rates are going to be determined primarily by the financial markets rather than by the arbitrary policy of central bankers, who will have limited flexibility, in particular over longer time horizons. As such, to understand how interest rates are likely to behave under a gold standard, we simply focus on our basic concepts of uncertainty and time preference and layer these over a reasonable trend growth rate assumption.

If we stick with an assumption of an underlying trend growth rate of around 3 percent but assume regular fluctuations around this of up to, say, 4 percent, then the economy will grow normally at rates ranging from mild contractions of −1 percent to occasional periods of up to 7 percent annual growth. Naturally, when growth expectations are around this elevated level, there will be strong demand for funds to invest, and interest rates will rise accordingly, most probably by a comparable magnitude. Conversely, when expectations are for a period of stagnation or recession, then savings rates will plummet to below 3 percent and might, from time to time, converge on zero.

While under a fiat currency regime, in which some degree of monetary inflation is the order of the day, zero rates might seem highly counterintuitive and result only from the arbitrary actions of central bankers setting rates, under a gold standard, in which material monetary inflation becomes all but impossible, extremely low interest rates, approaching zero, would be normal during periods of economic stagnation or recession.

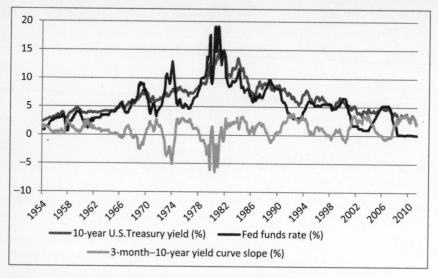

Figure 13.2   U.S. Fed Funds, 10-Year U.S. Treasury Yield Curve Slope
Source: Federal Reserve.

One important conclusion to draw, regarding the slope of the yield curve, is that absent the uncertainty associated with inflation, the term premium demanded by investors to hold longer-dated paper will decline dramatically, absent signs of rising fiscal deficits. As unsustainable fiscal deficits are the ultimate source of major inflations and devaluations versus other currencies or gold, naturally these would have an observable impact on term premiums under a gold standard.

As seen in Figure 13.2, business cycles have been the primary driver of yield curve slope. On average, the spread between Fed funds and the 10-year U.S. Treasury note yield has been around 2 percent. Under a credible gold standard, the volatility of the spread is not only likely to be lower—as a gold standard implies greater economic stability generally—but also the slope is likely to be somewhat less. The yield curve is also likely to invert more frequently.

CHAPTER 14

Estimating Risk Premia
under a Gold Standard

"[Via inflation] they create an abundance of disposable money for which its owners try to find the most profitable investment. Very promptly these funds find outlets in the stock exchange or in fixed investment. The notion that it is possible to pursue a credit expansion without making stock prices rise and fixed investment expand is absurd."
—Ludwig von Mises, *Human Action*, Chapter 31, Section 5

Interest rates are the fundamental valuation building block common to all assets. Future cash flows must be discounted at some rate to calculate a net present value, or estimated market price, for an asset. Where assets are not risk-free, however, as is the case with government bonds or any theoretical income stream with zero default risk, then the cash flows themselves must be estimated, as they are uncertain in both nominal and real terms. In this chapter, we consider how various risk premia are likely to be affected by the return to gold.

Risk Premia Where Cash Flows Are Fairly Certain

In cases where the degree of future cash flow uncertainty is relatively low, such as with investment-grade corporate bonds, risk premia tend to be rather small. It is highly unlikely that a mature business in a stable industry with low financial leverage is going to default on its debts. As such, the prices of investment-grade corporate bonds normally move closely in line with those of government bonds. Any spread of the corporate bond yield above that for a comparable-maturity government bond reflects the credit risk of the former, that is, the risk of default and the implied recovery rate on the firm's assets, should that occur.

None of this is going to change under a gold standard. As private-sector entities, corporations will always be at some risk of default. This risk needs to be priced into their bonds in the form of a yield spread over a corresponding risk-free asset such as a government bond. As the risk of default increases, so does the yield spread.

Corporate bond spreads must also incorporate assumed recovery rates. As the assumed recovery rate on defaulted corporate bonds decreases, the yield spread over risk-free bonds must increase to compensate investors for this risk.

In the case of unsecured bonds for complex multinational companies, recovery rates can be highly uncertain, of course. But this is true of a great many things in finance. While under a gold standard, inflation risk essentially disappears, other forms of risk remain. With corporate bonds, as well as other assets for which the future cash flows are to some degree uncertain, the risk premia implied in a yield spread or other discount to a risk-free benchmark reflect not inflation uncertainty but rather other, real economic forms of uncertainty, for example, the business cycle. In the long-term chart of U.S. corporate bond spreads in Figure 14.1, the impact of the business cycle is clear.

However, whereas with government bonds, inflation uncertainty would show up as a nominal yield in excess of real, with corporate or other assets at risk of default, inflation risk would, in fact, reduce the relative risk premium. This is because, absent a gold standard, a central bank is able to lower interest rates, create new money, fuel inflation, and also, if necessary, act as a lender of last resort such that, in the event of a sharp economic downturn, corporate default becomes rather less likely. Indeed, there is a natural bias for policymakers to act in this way, absent the constraint imposed by a gold standard. As Ludwig von Mises put it in his magnum opus, Human Action:

> [Money] expansion produces first the illusory appearance of prosperity. It is extremely popular because it seems to make the

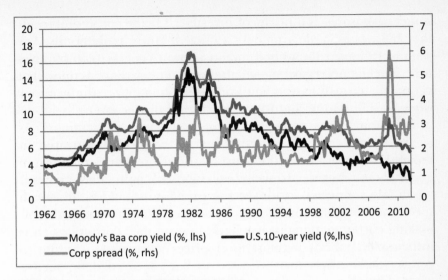

Figure 14.1   U.S. Corporate Bond Yields and Spreads
Source: Moody's, U.S. Federal Reserve.

majority, even everybody, more affluent. It has an enticing quality. A special moral effort is needed to stop it. On the other hand, contraction immediately produces conditions which everybody is ready to condemn as evil. Its unpopularity is even greater than the popularity of expansion. It creates violent opposition. Very soon the political forces fighting it become irresistible.[1]

As we will discuss shortly, this ability to manipulate interest rates to reduce or prevent corporate bankruptcies is not necessarily good news for an economy at large, as it prevents so-called "creative destruction" from taking place. However, from the perspective of an investor in a corporate bond, knowing that a central bank stands ready to create money to soften a downturn is seen as a reason for demanding a smaller risk premium over debt that is perceived as free of default risk, such as a government bond.

Other factors being equal, therefore, we should anticipate that corporate credit spreads would be wider under a gold standard than under a fiat standard. But it would be a mistake to conclude that

---

[1]Ludwig von Mises, *Human Action* (New Haven, CT: Yale University Press, 1949), Chapter 20, Section 7.

somehow business is fundamentally riskier. On the contrary, it means that businesses' access to debt capital markets is determined by a more rational, disciplined, market-driven process than by investors' speculation regarding whether and under what circumstances central banks will ease credit conditions to support the economy when certain firms, industries, or the entire economy is at risk of recession.

What holds for unsecured corporate bonds will also hold for secured. Recovery rates on bonds secured on specified assets are generally much easier to determine, and risk premia are generally much lower. But here, too, the risk premium should be higher. In the same way that central banks act to create inflation, thereby making corporate defaults less likely in economic downturns, these inflationary policies support asset prices generally, including, of course, those assets that are used to back secured debt, such as receivables of some kind and specified plant or equipment.

What holds for secured and unsecured corporate bonds also holds for non-risk-free assets generally. Under a gold standard, risk premia will be higher, other factors being equal. But they will be at a level that corresponds to the real risk assumed by economic actors, rather than distorted by the moral hazard of an implied bailout by a central bank easing monetary conditions. As such, capital is less likely to be misallocated. Firms or industries that get into trouble will spend less time trying to convince policy makers to bail them out and more time considering how best to restructure their operations to return to profitability. They may not always succeed in doing so, but then that is what Schumpeterian creative destruction is all about.

Risk Premia Where Cash Flows Are Fairly Uncertain

As one moves along the risk spectrum, from relatively safe investment-grade corporate bonds toward speculative-grade bonds, distressed debt, or equities, the risk premium increases. As such, the sensitivity of such assets to the monetary regime also increases. An implied bailout, in the form of artificially low interest rates, can have a dramatic impact on the equity risk premium, for example. As equities are claims on after-tax corporate profits, which tend to grow with inflation, the existence of a credible bailout for firms at risk of default can result in a dramatically lower risk premium. From an

Josef Schumpeter and Creative Destruction

Although not always associated with the Austrian Economic School, Josef Schumpeter was a student of a prominent Austrian economist, Eugen von Boehm-Bawerk, and a contemporary of both von Mises and von Hayek. He is best known for developing his concept of creative destruction, whereby inefficient firms, industries, or even entire economies must, from time to time, undergo periods of economic hardship to reorganize and restructure themselves to adapt to major changes in the underlying economic environment, including the adoption of new technologies that might threaten a dominant firm's market position, a successful industry's profit margins, or an entire economy's competitive advantage vis-à-vis other economies. As old factories are retooled and old industries die and new ones spring up, capital must necessarily be reallocated from one place to another, as fresh capital cannot be conjured out of thin air in the way money can be printed.

Indeed, this is one way to understand why inflation can be so harmful to economies in the long run, even if the rate is low and does not cause visible economic damage. What remains unseen is that, by creating money out of thin air, a central bank slows the capital reallocation and reorganization process. Firms or industries supported by easy money may be able to resist pressure to modernize or rationalize their operations for years. In the meantime, the entire economy forgoes the opportunity to restructure more aggressively, suffering a recession in the interim perhaps, but then recovering strongly at a higher sustainable growth rate with the advantages of younger, more dynamic firms; new technologies; and workers who have acquired the new skills required to implement them accordingly.

This need to destroy in order to create led Schumpeter to use the term *creative destruction* to describe this important aspect of capitalism. In doing so, he showed how what happens at the micro, firm-specific, and even worker-specific level of an economy cannot be separated from the macro. Monetary and fiscal policy might be used to reduce the volatility of the economic cycle, something that the modern economic mainstream considers sensible, but Schumpeter argued that healthy capitalist economies were arguably more volatile by their very nature, with boom-and-bust cycles serving a critical purpose by creating regular opportunities for creative destruction and, hence, real economic progress. Hubristic central bankers claiming credit for moderating business cycles should take note.

investors' point of view, if profits are to grow with inflation, on the one hand, yet default is highly unlikely, on the other, then there is practically no downside to equity investment, whereas by holding bonds instead, the investor receives little, if any, implied protection from monetary inflation.

This asymmetric risk profile perhaps explains why, during much of the 1990s and through the mid-2000s, observed equity risk premia have been generally lower than during the 1950s through the 1980s, notwithstanding frequently healthier economic growth during those former decades. Indeed, this apparent policy-driven compression of the equity risk premium in the 1990s through mid-2000s is so significant that it deserves a thorough examination. To do so, we will apply a classic valuation methodology, that of the capital asset pricing model (CAPM).

Using CAPM to Reveal How Inflation Distorts Asset Prices

Recall our previous discussion of the time value of money: It is to financial asset pricing what the speed of light is to Einstein's theories of relativity: While not a constant in the physical sense, the time value of money, as represented by the term structure of interest rates, is the universal point of reference for discounting the future cash flows on which financial assets represent legal claims.

Financial asset valuation models are therefore sensitive to interest rate assumptions, in particular when the cash flows are (1) relatively far out in the future and (2) relatively certain. The shorter the time and the more uncertain the cash flows, the less sensitive a financial asset price is to changes in the term structure of interest rates.

To illustrate this point, consider two financial assets: a long-term government bond and a lottery ticket for tomorrow's $10 million draw. As the cash flows accruing to the government bond are known in advance and extend far out into the future, the price of the bond is highly sensitive to changes in the term structure of interest rates. However, even a large change in interest rates does not have much impact on the value of the lottery ticket. Not only is the cash flow only one day away—not enough time for interest to accrue—but also it is unknown.

Probability theory can estimate the value of the lottery ticket, but, in practice, the payoff is so uncertain—a binary outcome of either zero or $10 million—that the actual value of the ticket is really just a function of statistical probability, independent of the term structure of interest rates.

Imagine now that the relative certainties of financial asset cash flows are laid out on a spectrum, from the certain to the highly uncertain. It might look something like this:

$$\text{Certain GBs} = \text{CBs} = \text{VEs} = \text{GEs} = \text{VC Uncertain}$$

where

      GBs = government bonds

      CBs = corporate bonds

      VEs = value equities

      GEs = growth equities

      VC = venture capital

As you move from left to right and the uncertainty of the realized size of the cash flows becomes ever greater, the present values (prices) of the cash flows become gradually less sensitive to the term structure of interest rates. As such, investments in equities and venture capital might seem to be relatively insensitive to interest rates. However, it is frequently the case that when it comes to investments in growth equities and venture capital, the cash flows that really matter—that determine whether the investment is going to outperform—are those at least a few years out in the future, perhaps even a decade or more. Due to the long duration of these cash flows, it would be a mistake to conclude that, just because they are relatively uncertain, these assets should not nevertheless be somewhat sensitive to interest rate assumptions.

Half a century ago, several economists working independently developed the key elements of the CAPM, which has provided a theoretical basis for risky-asset valuation models up to the present day.[2]

[2]William Sharpe, Henry Markowitz, and Merton Miller jointly received the 1990 Nobel Prize in Economics for the CAPM and modern portfolio theory (MPT), with which it is closely associated, although several others also did essential work in this area. William Sharpe is also well-known for his eponymous measure of risk-adjusted returns. In recent years, CAPM and MPT have come under increased scrutiny in part because they assume that financial market risk is normally distributed. The 2008–2009 credit crisis is just the latest example that this is not the case, although it may appear so from time to time. Recall that we discussed this at some length in Chapter 4.

In its simplest form, the CAPM model calculates the expected return of a financial asset according to the following equation:

$$E(R_i) = R_f + B_i[E(R_m) - R_f]$$

where

$E(R_i)$ = expected rate of return

R_f = risk-free interest rate

B_i = sensitivity (risk) of the asset relative to the market for comparably risky assets

$E(R_m)$ = expected return of the market for comparably risky assets

While it is obvious that the interest rate R_f plays a role here, notice that, as the measures of risk B_i or $E(R_m)$ approach zero, the expected return on the asset becomes a function entirely of the risk-free interest rate, normally assumed to be that on government bonds. But as B_i and $E(R_m)$ rise, the expected return on the asset becomes less dependent on the risk-free interest rate. If, alternatively, $E(R_m)$ is highly uncertain, the risk-free rate also becomes less relevant.

Regardless, note how the model is based entirely on the concept of relative value: Assets are being valued relative to a risk-free asset and relative to the market for comparably risky assets. Now given that interest rate assumptions have at least a modest impact on relative risky asset valuations, note that if the risk-free rate R_f is being held artificially low by the monetary authority, then this has the effect of increasing the expected returns on risky assets relative to risk-free assets. In other words, risky assets in general will become fundamentally overvalued.

Applied to corporate bonds, this implies that, even absent any explicit or implied government support, spreads to government bonds will become too tight to compensate investors for the fundamental risks they are taking, as we showed earlier in this chapter. And risky equities will become overvalued relative to bonds and to low-beta (low-risk) equities.

This implies that, for any given level of future earnings assumptions, equity P/E ratios will be higher than they would otherwise be, such that investors end up paying more for shares than they can reasonably expect to get back (someday) in the form of actual, after-tax, discounted earnings. By implication, were interest rates allowed to adjust to their natural equilibrium, corporate credit spreads would most likely rise, and share P/Es fall.

Leaving the fundamentals aside for the moment, some might argue that stock market investment is not necessarily investment at all but rather a form of speculation and that what stock market speculators are after is short-term capital gains rather than value-based long-term earnings growth. Warren Buffett and other successful value investors would beg to differ. But Buffett would probably be among the first to acknowledge that a substantial portion of stock market transactions represent the whims of speculators rather than the careful, systematic, value-driven determinations of sensible, value-oriented investors. Indeed, it is the actions of the speculators that move prices to levels that are fundamentally unjustified, which create the very opportunities that value investors such as Buffett seek to exploit.

How Distorting Interest Rates Causes Real Economic Damage

This discussion leads us to another way in which the actions of the monetary authority can become so detrimental to the economy at large. By making it more difficult to value risky assets properly and by generally inflating the value of such assets beyond what fundamentals can justify, value-driven investors will be less willing to invest in the market generally. Investment flows will become increasingly dominated by those who are really just speculating and chasing trends rather than making reasoned judgments about which companies offer the best potential long-term value.

But the stock market does not exist in a vacuum. The valuations placed on stocks represent the abilities of companies to raise capital in the form of new shares or debt issues, to acquire other companies through merger or acquisition, to compensate their employees with shares or options—in a word, to grow. If the stock market becomes overvalued, companies are liable to overinvest in their operations.

If speculators rather than value investors are the primary force behind stock price trends, then economic resources generally are being allocated in an inefficient, haphazard way that leads to malinvestments. Such malinvestments, over time, have the effect of reducing the overall economy's potential growth rate, as they divert resources from more productive activities or,

(Continued)

alternatively, lead to a general overinvestment in the capital stock such that depreciation becomes a drag on growth.[3]

Consider the tech bubble for example. Notwithstanding the very real technological advances taking place in the 1990s, by 1997 the stock prices of tech firms began to rise out of line with any reasonable assumptions of economic reality. Value investors began to retreat from the market, leaving it more open to speculators. In the wake of the Asian crisis in 1997, which reduced the attractiveness of emerging markets, these speculators moved more aggressively into tech stocks. When the Fed bailed out Long-Term Capital Management (LTCM) in 1998 and also eased monetary conditions briefly going into Y2K, speculators became even more aggressive. As tech and other stock prices rose and rose, these companies spent more and more on various expansion plans.

Eventually, it all came crashing down, and the malinvestments were exposed for what they were. Sure, there were real economic advances that had taken place, but valuations, with much help from the Fed, had become so stretched that a bust became inevitable. To compensate for that bust, of course, the Fed eased policy even more aggressively than it had in the wake of the LTCM failure, with the entirely predictable consequence that new bubbles would form elsewhere, this time in residential and commercial real estate and in global credit markets generally, leading to even greater malinvestments, which have subsequently been exposed as such by a commensurately greater bust. As for where the next bubbles are now forming, we believe that the Fed and economic policy makers generally have spun a vast web of financial market distortions and systemic moral hazard that facilitates asset misallocations just about everywhere. Financial history may not repeat, but it certainly rhymes.

A More Robust CAPM: Valuing Financial Assets as Options

Our discussion of valuations so far has been based on a classic interpretation of what qualifies as a risk premium and how it can be imputed from observed financial asset prices and a benchmark risk-free interest rate. There are robust ways of estimating risk premia,

---

[3]It may seem counterintuitive that a capital stock can become too large. After all, the greater the capital stock, the greater the overall productive potential of the economy. But consider: If the capital stock grows relative to the level of the available labor to service and maintain it correctly, then it will depreciate prior to being utilized fully to produce consumer goods, resulting in a net loss of wealth. Just as economies can overconsume, they can also overinvest if interest rates are held at artificially low levels. Take a look at the many empty U.S. homes left in the wake of defaulted mortgages, depreciating away, and this loss of wealth can be observed directly.

however. One of these is to value assets based on the implied option-ality of future cash flows.

As mentioned previously, some cash flows are less certain than others. Where cash flows are uncertain, however, one can make the assumption that they are likely to fit a distribution. Classic option pricing theory assumes a Gaussian, or normal, bell-curve shaped distribution for financial variables. The original options pricing model, which became the basis for the growth of the derivatives industry in the 1980s, was published in 1973 by Fischer Black and Myron Scholes and is known as the Black-Scholes model.

Black and Scholes set out to show that, using Gaussian distribution assumptions, one could place an objective value on randomly distributed outcomes, including movements in stock prices and other financial assets. But one can take a similar set of assumptions and apply it to the cash flows that comprise the given valuation of a financial asset.

Take an oil well, for example, that can produce a barrel of oil for a cost of $80. Naturally, as long as the price of oil exceeds $80 per barrel, the well turns a profit. Should the price of oil decline below $80, however, it is not profitable to operate the well. As such, the well represents the option to produce oil and should be valued as such: Rather than just assuming an average future price of oil and discounting the implied future cash flows at some risk-free rate to determine the net present value of the well today, it is a more robust process to assume a distribution for the future oil price and to value the well as an *option* to produce oil instead.

Viewed in this way, all productive assets are options. Some might not be as easy as an oil well to turn on or off. But if price swings are large and sustained enough, even the most complex industrial pro-cesses are, ultimately, options rather than obligations to produce something.

An investor applying an options-based valuation methodology could possibly determine, for example, that a mature company in a relatively stable industry, was overvalued relative to a younger, riskier competitor. Whereas investors generally prefer stable investments to less stable ones, the implied option value of certain risky operations could, in theory, make the riskier firms more attractive.

This becomes particularly possible, of course, if the riskier firms are perceived as having some form of implied bailout in the form of a proactive central bank easing of policy in response to economic downturns. In this sense, even the disciplined, value-based investor, looking at cash flows from the bottom up, and applying options-based valuation techniques, ends up making investment decisions that are influenced by the central bank, valuing risky enterprises at an artificial premium to less risky ones, thereby misallocating capital in the process, to the broader economy's detriment.

Beyond CAPM: Valuing Assets in a Nonnormal World

As explored at length in Part I, much modern financial theory, including the hugely influential CAPM valuation methodology, and actual practice, is based on Gaussian, normal distribution assumptions. While certainly convenient from a risk calculation perspective, such assumptions are also convenient for those who desire to take excessive risk in investment decisions. Regardless of which motivating factor explains the lingering dominance of Gaussian finance, for years a growing number of prominent intellectuals have been pointing out that financial asset returns are emphatically not normally distributed but follow rather scale-invariant power curve distributions, as described by Jim Rickards in Chapter 4.

The father of the anti-Gaussian rebellion in modern finance was no doubt the late Benoit Mandelbrot. Although he came rather late to finance, his work was to have a profound intellectual impact. Mandelbrot demonstrated that the financial world only appeared Gaussian to observers ensconced within a cave in which financial crises simply did not occur or were deliberately removed from the data set outright, as exceptional events. But of course, we know they occur. They occur across time, across economies, and across cultures, and they occur with a frequency completely out of line with Gaussian assumptions.

What Mandelbrot discovered was the fractal nature of financial markets. That is, what happens frequently on a small scale occurs infrequently on a large scale. The scale itself is determined by the size of the financial system. Other factors being equal, as the system grows in size, so does the potential future crisis. Like earthquakes, these crises cannot be predicted with respect to timing. Their size, however, can be estimated and capital provisioned against anticipated future losses.

Why is this important to our discussion of risk premia? Recall that the implied bailout of the financial system and economy generally by central banks depresses risk premia to artificially low levels. This in turn implies that too much risk is taken; that is, the financial system and economy grow excessively in size through leverage. From time to time, a generally unforeseen development takes place that exposes that the risk provisioning in the system is inadequate, and a general crash ensues. At this point, the central bank can be relied on to do as it has done before and bail out the system yet again, encouraging it to grow even bigger in the future, thereby sowing the seeds of the next crisis, and so on.

Under a gold standard, this escalating boom-and-bust process becomes impossible, as it becomes prohibitively costly for economic agents to hold misplaced Gaussian assumptions. Low-risk premia that do not reflect reality lead to failed enterprises, plain and simple. There will be no bailout. Financial risk premia will reflect the non-Gaussian reality of the world in which we actually live, not the cave in which the economic mainstream resides, continuing to assume as if financial crises are some sort of aberration.

By implication, under a gold standard, risk premia will be higher. Equity and risky-asset valuations will therefore rise, other factors being equal, relative to their less risky alternatives. Value-driven investing, itself infected by the moral hazard of the current fiat dollar global monetary regime, will heal itself with proper, Mandelbrot-inspired, real-world assumptions and will largely, although never completely, displace more speculative forms of investing in which short-term traders attempt to offload fundamentally overvalued assets on others before they are exposed by future events as such.

This is yet another way in which the return to gold will be salutary for the global economy. There will be a renaissance of disciplined, value-based investing and a decline in speculation. Financial firms will be forced to greatly derisk their balance sheets, as will highly leveraged corporations that attract capital because of implied bailout speculation rather than by representing superior fundamental value. Notwithstanding the net benefits, the return to gold will thus produce both winners and losers, and it to this that we now turn.

CHAPTER 15

Golden Winners and Paper Losers

The financial sector of our economy is the largest profit-making sector in America. . . . We've become a financial economy, which has overwhelmed the productive economy.
—John Bogle, CEO of Vanguard Fund Management, interview with Bill Moyers, September 2007

When considering which firms, industries, and asset classes are likely to benefit or suffer most in relative terms from a return to gold, we need to focus on fundamental value rather than speculation. We also must not lose sight of the role that risk-premium adjustments are likely to play. In general, the better-performing assets will be those that will see the smallest increases in risk premia, as risk premia in general are likely to rise somewhat as a trade-off for the disappearance of the inflation risk premium from the scene.

Should the transition period to gold prove disorderly, history suggests that valuations may reach levels that are extremely depressed. Yes, earnings are likely to rise in nominal terms if there is a general surge in global inflation associated with the decline in the purchasing power of the dollar and fiat currencies generally. But in real terms, they may not rise at all and could well decline, as global growth is likely to be weak. The rise in economic uncertainty, in general, is likely to favor defensive assets, albeit those that cannot simply be devalued through inflation, such as fixed-interest securities, including, of course, government bonds.

Within equities, which do offer some protection from inflation, value-based investing should do better than growth. High dividend yields will command a valuation premium. Firms providing stable products, services, and infrastructure and offering some global diversification should fare relatively well, but total market equity P/E ratios in the single digits are likely to be observed once it appears that the transition to gold is relatively certain and the temporary surge in inflation and future expectations thereof begin to subside. Should that seem overly bearish to some, consider that the U.S. equity market traded at a single-digit P/E ratio in the early 1980s, the last time there was serious speculation that the United States might be headed back to a gold standard.

What applies to firms, industries, and asset classes also applies to entire countries and financial systems. Notwithstanding massive global linkages, some economies and financial systems are less leveraged than others, and these are likely to fare relatively better following the return to gold.

Financials

Nowhere is the adjustment back to a gold standard going to be as significant as within the financial system itself. It follows that the valuation of financial firms is going to change dramatically. As it turns out, this will not be for the better. Arguably, the single biggest financial market implication of a return to gold will be a general derating of financial corporate assets to nonfinancial.

First, consider that the implied bailout in place under the current fiat dollar standard applies first and foremost to the too-big-to-fail firms that reside at the center of the financial system. It is here that risk is concentrated and where risk premia are artificially most compressed relative to those elsewhere. A return to gold will reduce and possibly eliminate the entire too-big-to-fail advantage. By implication, there will be a large relative rise in risk premia in this sector.

Second, consider how financial firms have grown their earnings through various forms of financial engineering that have allowed excessive leverage into the system. Following a return to gold, much of this financial engineering will be seen to be superfluous. Much of what happens in finance is related to the origination and subsequent hedging of interest rate risk. As we have shown, much interest rate risk is generated by inflation and expectations thereof.

By essentially eliminating the risk of inflation, these activities will become unnecessary and uneconomic.

The ability of the financial system to grow faster than the economy generally, as has been the underlying trend since the dollar's link to gold was severed, will be thrown into reverse. At best, financial firms' profits will keep up with the economy but only after a painful period of downsizing. Originating and then retiring financial instruments only to the extent that these transactions support real economic activity should not be a particularly high-margin business and, absent leverage, should generate reasonable but hardly spectacular profits. Investors anticipating a return to gold should therefore strategically underweight financial shares and also their riskier, subordinated debt.

Industrials

Unlike financial firms, which have been the primary beneficiaries of the fiat dollar reserve standard, industrial firms have been only indirectly affected. Yes, they, too, have enjoyed structurally lower risk premia as a result of the general implied economic bailout provided by the monetary authorities, but to a much lesser extent. As such, while their risk premia are likely to be higher under a gold standard than at present, the relative increase is likely to be far smaller.

It could be argued that the real outperformers following a return to gold would be industrial corporate bonds. While they, too, will see higher risk premia under a gold standard than is the case today, the increase will be slight in comparison to that for corporate shares and for financial companies' bonds. However, the transition back to gold is likely to be temporarily highly inflationary, as we discussed in Part II. As fixed-interest securities, industrial corporate bonds are thus not likely to fare as well as shares during the transition phase. But once the return to gold is complete, there is a strong probability that corporate bonds will, in general, enjoy a period of relative outperformance.

One way to get exposure to the industrial bond sector without taking as much inflation risk is to buy floating-rate notes (FRNs). When inflation rises as the world transitions back to gold, so will the coupons of floating-rate notes. Yet the risk premia associated with FRNs should rise by less than that for industrial companies' shares, for the very same reason as for corporate bonds in general. As such, industrial FRNs, in particular for strong, investment-grade firms, provide investors with an excellent way to avoid the risk premium expansion and temporary inflation risks that are likely to characterize the transition period back to gold.

Industrial Subsectors

Within industrials, some sectors are likely to perform better than others during the transition back to gold. Here we take a look at a few sectors that are likely to be most affected.

Mining

An obvious candidate for outperformance is the precious metals mining sector, the valuation of which is a direct function of the price of precious metals. That said, investors must take into account other factors in this sector, in particular the speculative element presented by immature mines or exploration activities, but when it comes to reliable, established operations, it follows that a rise in the price of precious metals leads to rising miners' share prices.

As it stands at the time I am writing, however, due to a generally poor performance by global stock markets over the past year, the share prices of major precious metals mining firms, in particular those that employ leverage, are unusually low relative to gold and silver. As such, it could be argued that investors looking to profit from a return to gold should consider an allocation to established gold- and silver-mining firms.

So-called junior miners may struggle to perform as well. In principle, they provide investors with more leverage. However, as risk premia in general expand under a gold standard, relatively riskier mining and exploration operations may see their relative valuations suffer for a time. Once the transition back to gold is complete, however, and the global economy stabilizes, then it is highly likely that the junior miners will offer a range of enticing opportunities, albeit with more risk than their mature counterparts.

Consumer Nondiscretionary

It stands to reason that staple products are likely to remain in demand no matter how disruptive the transition back to gold proves to be.

Defensive investors normally overweight this sector, and for good reason. Not only is demand relatively stable but also it is generally assumed that consumer staple product prices rise with inflation.

The downside, of course, is that the sector normally presents less opportunity for robust growth. But during the transition back to gold, robust growth will remain elusive in many economies.

Although long out of favor, food production, processing, transport, and storage are basic, generally low-risk businesses that represent arguably the most staple of all staple products: nutrition. During the potentially disorderly and inflationary transition back to gold, there is certainly still going to be demand for food. Food infrastructure in general is going to remain absolutely essential, no matter how much disruption there is to the financial system and other industries. Food prices are also likely to rise more or less in line with any interim surge in inflation as gold is revalued and the dollar devalued.

Once the transition period is complete, however, the safe haven aspects of this sector will become relatively less attractive. There will probably remain selective opportunities in certain foods and in certain parts of the world that are becoming more affluent and consuming more and higher-quality food, with higher protein content.

Consumer Discretionary

While normally riskier than consumer nondiscretionary shares, during the potentially highly disruptive transition back to gold, there is likely to be a considerably larger expansion of risk premia for discretionary relative to nondiscretionary shares. Amid huge uncertainty and, for many, loss of purchasing power, discretionary purchases will be postponed.

Demand for durable goods, such as automobiles and appliances, will be particularly hard hit. In addition to the factors just mentioned, these purchases are frequently financed. Like financing activities generally, as any implied bailout essentially disappears and financial risk premia expand under a gold standard, it will become more expensive for households to fund purchases on credit.

It is worth considering, however, how this reduction in demand for durable goods will affect certain other activities. As consumers delay purchasing new vehicles or appliances, for example, they are going to need to extend the practical working lives of those they already have. Specialty producers of replacement parts and providers of servicing and improvements or upgrades that can be applied to existing vehicles and appliances are likely to be in relatively stronger demand. Indeed, any means of maintaining the existing capital stock for less cost should be in good demand during the transition to gold.

Capital Goods

As is the case with consumer durables, the transition back to gold is likely to see a general underperformance of capital goods shares. Naturally, such shares are highly cyclical. Also, these firms tend to have large R&D costs that are recovered only over long periods of time. In some cases, capital goods producers make a profit only from the maintenance, servicing, and provision of spare parts for their equipment, such as with aircraft engines, for example. In certain cases, capital goods producers have financing arms that assist customers with the term financing of these expensive purchases. Like financing activities generally, however, these will be less profitable under a gold standard.

Once the transition is complete, however, and financing activities have shrunk to a more appropriate size, this is one of the sectors that will benefit most from the migration of capital out of financing activities generally and back into the real, productive economy. The loss of engineering talent in the financial sector will be a huge gain for the industrial sector generally, including capital goods.

Utilities

Long regarded as a staid, uninteresting business, utilities may provide one of the most interesting areas for investment, both during the transition back to gold and subsequently. As mature, generally defensive companies, with relatively high dividend yields, they have the basic characteristics that we have identified as most suitable for outperformance during the potentially disorderly transition back to a gold standard. However, they are also an area ripe for innovation.

Among industrial sectors, utilities are the most heavily regulated. In many cases, they are either owned outright by the government or the government owns a large stake. Many are regulated monopolies, ultimately run by politicians who generally do not seek to maximize shareholder value.

Under a gold standard, in which government involvement in the economy is almost certain to be somewhat less, there exists the potential for substantial deregulation of utilities. The increased potential for innovation as capital is redirected from the financial sector and the arrival of new engineering talent could result in substantial technological innovation and increased efficiency. Profit margins could increase substantially.

While no doubt utilities would become riskier investments in this scenario, the increase in risk would be longer term, after the return to a credible gold standard had already been achieved. As such, they would most likely retain their safe haven status in the interim.

Technology

As such a huge part of the global economy, the technology sector has become increasingly difficult to treat as a single entity for valuation. However, we can offer a few general thoughts.

First, as with capital goods producers, technology firms will benefit hugely from the migration of both capital and skilled labor from the financial sector. There might well be a surge in technological innovation as a result, although it might take some years for that to materialize.

Second, during the transition period, chances are that there will be relatively less demand for new technological infrastructure. This is particularly true for consumer electronics, which represents technology for consumption rather than for productive investment. As such, for the transition period, investors should focus on those technologies that generally help to keep down industrial production costs rather than those designed to appeal directly to consumers in the form of discretionary products.

Some Thoughts on Investment Diversification

It is often said that diversification is the only free lunch in economics. As such, investors should always prefer more, to the extent that diversification does not adversely affect investment returns over time, say by diversifying into chronically poor investments.

In recent years, as financial markets have become almost exclusively focused on policy makers' actions from one day to the next, as one crisis after another escalates, then calms down, then escalates unexpectedly yet again, financial asset prices have become unusually highly correlated. As the source for most volatility in expectations for growth, inflation, and economic variables generally now resides with the highly activist policy-making community, rather than at a firm- or industry-specific level, it is only natural that the expected fortunes of a given firm or industry rise or fall more or less together. Put another way, the bulk of the risk in the world is now primarily systematic rather than idiosyncratic. As such, there is far, far less diversification to be had in financial assets generally.

Even commodity prices are now unusually highly correlated to financial markets, although substantially less so than the correlations between financial assets themselves. The point is that the growth in what is quite clearly centralized economic planning, as opposed to firm- or industry-specific initiative, has created an unusually binary investment outlook.

While symptomatic of the final stage of the global experiment of a fiat currency reserve standard and associated asset bubbles and busts, this presents investors not only with a tremendous challenge but also with an opportunity. Where diversification can be found, it is likely to find unusually good investment demand. It may take a substantial amount of detective work, but the new firm, new industry, new technology, or applications thereof in a new region or country naturally still provide investors with opportunities for diversification at reasonable valuations. No matter how disorderly the transition to gold becomes, there will always be a role for traditional, value-based investing to play in any disciplined investment process.

CHAPTER 16

Some Implications of the Gold Standard for Global Labor and Capital Markets

> [P]olicies about trade and finance should have as their objective the maximum possible free trade in goods and services and free movement of capital . . . [A] relatively stable price level . . . will generally promote that objective.[1]
> —Nobel laureate Milton Friedman, 2001

It is important to give some consideration to the implications of the gold standard for global labor and capital markets, in the highly likely event that the bulk of the globe returns to a gold standard. For example, just because one region might be in recession does not imply that others are, notwithstanding the strong global economic linkages observed today. There will always be regional economic differences, in particular between countries with highly distinct economic characteristics, such as agrarian economies, those associated with mining activities, or those primarily engaged in manufacturing or financial services.

We have seen how, under a gold standard, financial markets, rather than central banks, will ultimately determine the level of interest rates. But in a global economy, characterized by global capital flows, the level of interest rates will be determined by global supply and global demand, not local. As such, even if the rate

---

[1] "One World, One Money," *Options Politiques/Policy Options*, May 2001.

of growth approached zero in one part of the world, were other parts more dynamic, growing in excess of 3 percent, say, then gold would flow from where capital was not in demand to where it was, pulling interest rates in the relatively less dynamic regions higher or, at a minimum, preventing them from falling as much as they otherwise would.

This might seem suboptimal from the perspective of a weak economy. Wouldn't it be better if they had their own currency and central bank and could lower interest rates as required to support growth instead? Perhaps in the short term, yes. But consider: Naturally fluctuating interest rates function as an automatic stabilizing mechanism. Eventually, they rise to a level that prevents a further outflow of gold and implies a higher domestic savings rate. That savings then becomes available for investment, required for a sustainable economic recovery. Moreover, under a gold standard, wages and other variable costs become by necessity more flexible. If it is impossible to inflate or devalue one's way out of an economic downturn, then by implication, production costs must be flexible on the downside. As wages decline, the weaker economy becomes relatively more competitive internationally and the gold flows back in.

Capital, too, must be more flexible. If businesses are struggling to make a profit or begin to go bankrupt, then they will need to restructure. Money printing will not be available to bail out shareholders or bond-holders, who will be responsible for taking over failed enterprises, restructuring their operations, and perhaps breaking them into pieces and selling them off so that capital can be more efficiently employed elsewhere.

This process of labor and capital flexibility and mobility, corporate reorganization and renewal is absolutely essential to long-term economic progress. Without it, capital gets locked up in old, less dynamic businesses and outmoded technologies. Labor gets stuck in relatively poor, unproductive regions. Progress becomes more and more elusive. By resorting to lower interest rates and inflation, central banks repeatedly soften the short-term impact of an economic downturn. But there is no free lunch. In doing so, central banks prevent Schumpeterian "creative destruction" as described in Chapter 14: real economic restructuring, renewal, and long-term advancement. Economies become ossified as a consequence, fail either to develop new technologies or even to adopt those with proven advantages elsewhere.

Eventually, the gap between stagnant economies and those that allow for the occasional major restructuring becomes so vast that they are considered to exist in different "worlds", as in the "developed" and the "developing". Economic history provides numerous examples of this phenomenon. Recall that, as Europe was stagnating through the early Middle Ages, major economic advances were taking place in China and elsewhere in Asia, only to ultimately be suppressed by inflexible regimes.

However, given a sufficient level of flexibility, eventually a combination of higher rates on savings and lower wages makes labor more attractive and capital more available, precisely the combination that can lay the groundwork for a sound, sustainable economic recovery. Meanwhile, those economies that don't experience higher rates on savings or falling wages become less competitive over time, eventually yielding their dynamism to their previously less fortunate counterparts. Interest rates, so distorted by the chronic manipulations of policy makers under today's fiat standard, will better facilitate the efficient allocation of global capital flows under the coming global gold standard.

By implication of wages being necessarily more flexible, up and down, under a gold standard, in which inflationary responses to unemployment become for all practical purposes impossible to sustain, labor is likely, in general, to be more mobile. In large part, this will be due to the greater difficulty for governments in financing substantial unemployment benefits for an extended period. Labor will seek to move not only within borders to wherever the better jobs are but also, to the extent allowed by the authorities, across them. While picking up and moving, in particular across borders, can be hugely disruptive for households, it does serve an important economic purpose, both in limiting the duration of unemployment and, thinking longer-term, facilitating the movement of labor to where it can be most efficiently employed.

A thorough discussion of the apparent trade-off between economic flexibility on the one hand, and social continuity on the other, is beyond the scope of this book. However, in the conclusion which follows, I explore a number of the more significant social consequences of the coming golden revolution.

Conclusion: The Golden Society

I believe that banking institutions are more dangerous to our liberties than standing armies . . . If the American people ever allow private banks to control the issue of their currency, first by inflation, then by deflation, the banks and corporations that will grow up around [the banks] . . . will deprive the people of all property until their children wake-up homeless on the continent their fathers conquered . . . The issuing power should be taken from the banks and restored to the people, to whom it properly belongs.

—President Thomas Jefferson, speaking in opposition to the recharter of the Bank Bill (1809)

As we observed in Part II, a young Alan Greenspan, in his 1966 essay "Gold and Economic Freedom," published in Ayn Rand's *The Objectivist*, made the case for a return to a pure gold standard from the somewhat ambiguous Bretton Woods system in not only an economic sense but also a moral sense, in that gold ownership protects private property rights and, by implication, protects the individual against government tyranny. As such, he explicitly placed gold at the center of the entire Western, liberal philosophical tradition, tracing its way back to the Enlightenment. Indeed, the perennial debate between Hobbesian statists, on the one hand, and Lockean anarchists on the other, is to some extent resolved through gold: Not only does it provide for protection of private property rights, as Locke would have it, but also it provides a degree of objective economic order, providing a universal point of reference for society at large.

The U.S. founding fathers, including Thomas Jefferson, quoted above, sought to resolve this dilemma in practice with the drafting and ratification of the U.S. Constitution, which provided the federal government with a handful of enumerated powers. Among these was the power to coin money and regulate the value thereof. The first explicit exercise of this power, the Coinage act of 1792, defined the dollar as an exact weight of silver and gold. The Congress thus assumed its constitutional monetary authority in a way which prevented banks from somehow arbitrarily inflating (or, for that matter, deflating) the money supply.

Hobbes was concerned primarily about preventing a never-ending, anarchic "war of all against all" that would render the life of man "solitary, poor, nasty, brutish and short." As such, he believed an authoritarian state was indispensable. Yet he also understood that trade and commerce were essential to satisfying human needs and wants and to the general advancement of civilization. Along these lines, consider that by providing an objective, voluntary, universally accepted medium of exchange, gold has allowed individuals to trade more extensively with one another, outside the family or tribal unit. Absent gold or, alternatively, increasingly authoritarian, command-economy (e.g. communist) societies, there would be only pure barter and some degree of reciprocal altruism, greatly limiting the achievable division of labor and, hence, economic progress. The life of man would remain relatively poor and probably quite short.

It wouldn't necessarily be solitary, nasty or brutish, but history demonstrates that with increased trade, war tends to become less frequent. Sound money facilitates trade. As we saw in Part I, unstable money destabilizes trade. Unstable money thus threatens to undo the historically significant growth of world trade in recent decades, as indeed it did in Europe during and following World War I.

It is no coincidence that, following the world wars of the first half of the twentieth century, the gold-backed Western monetary order was restored, albeit in somewhat hegemonic fashion by the U.S., thereby facilitating trade and commerce. Elsewhere, absent stable money, economic modernization and trade growth, authoritarian regimes dominated.

With the collapse of the Soviet bloc in the 1990s came, on the one hand, the apparent triumph of the West, yet, on the other, the economic modernization and trade growth associated with progressively less-authoritarian regimes. As we have seen, the BRIC (Brazil, Russia, India, China) economies and smaller emerging markets now represent a large and growing part of the global economy. As such, mercantilist, growth-oriented policies in the developing world, supported by Western money and credit growth, have more than outlived their usefulness, as has the fiat dollar global reserve standard. They are now destabilizing the very economies they previously enabled to grow.

In a sense, the wheel has come full circle. With the erosion of authoritarianism around the world has come the rebalancing of economic power away from the hegemonic monetary order previously provided by the fiat dollar. As is often the case with history, it may seem ironic that in the triumph of the Western liberal economic and political traditions over authoritarianism lay the seeds of the fiat dollar's eventual demise. Yet it has always been gold, rather than an unbacked fiat currency, that has presided over a multipolar world, whether liberal or authoritarian.

A useful historical parallel with today might be the decline of Spain and the emergence of a multipolar European world in the early seventeenth century. As long as Spain remained the monetary hegemon, bringing a seemingly endless supply of gold and silver from the New World to Europe, it could finance wars on demand and dominate much of the continent, including the economically powerful low countries. Yet what seemed endless was anything but, and, as the mint gradually emptied out, Spain sued for peace and Europe's most destructive war to that point came to an end, to be followed by a century and a half of relative peace and growing prosperity, inaugurated by the Peace of Westphalia in 1648. (Incidentally, this relative peace came to an end with the French Revolution and eventual rise of Napoleon. In my opinion, it is no coincidence that the revolution against Louis XVI followed on a period of highly inflationary policies that were not curtailed but rather expanded by the revolutionaries. Large inflations tend to precede, to coincide with and to follow major wars and revolutions.)

Returning to the present, the hegemonic post–World War II economic order has long since given way to a more multipolar one. Now, following the global credit crisis that began in 2008, the already fragile fiat dollar reserve equilibrium has become terminally destabilized. Gold will thus soon resume its normal, historical role for a nonhegemonic, multipolar world of expanding trade.

We have already discussed at length some of the more important economic and financial market implications of a return to a gold standard. Along the way, we have occasionally touched on some associated societal implications. It remains to draw some firmer conclusions in this area.

Gold helps to protect private property rights, in particular by preventing governments from running deficits and other inflationary policies. If governments cannot confiscate property through deficit spending and inflation, they will be able to do so only through taxation. With each generation having to pay for government as it goes along, rather than passing that burden onto some number of future generations, it stands to reason that there will be greater scrutiny over government spending, which will more closely reflect societal preferences.

There is also a larger moral question here in whether it is right for one generation to borrow from another. I do not believe this to be the case absent a clear, present, existential danger to a society. Yet alongside the rise of the modern, deficit-funded welfare state has come a general acceptance of the immoral practice of leaving future generations with the bill for current consumption. A return to gold will put an end to that practice in short order.

In Part III, we touched on how labor and capital will necessarily be come more mobile under a gold standard, as policy makers will be less able to support poor economic regions at the expense of relatively affluent ones. While no doubt disruptive for a time, labor and capital mobility are part and parcel of Shumpeterian creative destruction, without which significant economic progress becomes all but impossible.

Once again, there is a moral argument to be made here: Is it right for people in one location to be subsidized indefinitely by people in another location just because the former cast a greater number of votes? This is akin to the majority voting to appropriate the wealth of the minority. Such a tyranny of the majority, so feared by the U.S. founding fathers and specifically addressed in the limited federal powers and various checks and balances of the U.S. Constitution, would not long last under a gold standard, in which uneconomic transfers of wealth would be met with an outflow of gold and higher interest rates.

But it is not just the tyranny of the majority that will be curtailed by a return to gold. Any organized group that seeks rents from the government in exchange for political contributions or votes will find it is up against stiffer opposition. With greater fiscal restraint implied by the tether of gold, there will be far fewer political favors to give away. Fewer favors will lead to less rent-seeking activity in the first place. Firms will spend less time lobbying governments and more time rationalizing their operations, developing and implementing new technologies, and so on, to the benefit of all.

As gold also protects wealth and prohibits its confiscation through inflation, the simple virtue of saving will be strengthened. While there will always be those inclined to speculate, no doubt some of whom get lucky and wealthy as a result, it is the simple saver who benefits most from gold, not the speculator. As we have seen, risk premia for financial assets in general are likely to be higher under a gold standard. This implies that, not only will savers be better compensated for saving, but also investors will be better compensated for the risks they take.

Yes, this may imply that corporate CEOs and other top executives find it more difficult to secure outsize pay packages for substandard performance, but a rebalancing of power from corporate insiders to shareholders will not only help to ensure that the owners of the corporations—the shareholders—are the primary beneficiaries of profit growth but also dissuade CEOs from excessive risk-taking, as it will become more difficult to extract huge payouts from a company, short of a long and successful tenure.

Looking at the financial sector specifically, in a noninflationary world with no implied bailout for financial firms, there will be far less financial risk appetite relative to the desire to take operational risk. Profits will migrate from financial to operational activities. And where profits migrate, so does capital and labor. Resources being poured into financial activities today will be poured into operational ones instead. Many of those engineers, scientists, mathematicians, and other intelligent, highly trained quants who were drawn to finance in recent years due to the apparent promise of huge salaries and bonuses will find their way into productive enterprises, seeking to build a better mousetrap, or widget, or whatever. Fresh graduates will join over time. Together, they will develop new technologies and run more efficient firms for the benefit of the broader economy.

Although we could go on, the list is already rather extensive: Gold protects private property and also political rights, by limiting the power of government to tax or inflate away the former, while constraining the government's ability to give away political favors to organized rent-seeking groups at the expense of the majority. Gold helps prevent one generation from taxing the next via excessive government borrowing; it helps prevent one region from taxing another just because it delivers more votes; it redirects resources

from financial speculation toward value-driven, productive investment; it helps to prevent insider abuse and control fraud from
wrecking otherwise profitable corporations; it returns the basic
virtues of thrift, savings, and good old-fashioned hard work to the
center of society, thereby strengthening the moral compass and
mutual trust required for the advancement of civilization.

The golden revolution thus promises to be not just monetary,
economic, and financial but also societal. And while the transition
may be painful for most, it will become only more so the longer it
is pushed back. We should therefore not only embrace gold-backed
money as arguably the best way to protect wealth in uncertain times;
we should embrace it as the best way to place the global economy
back on a sustainable path and, in so doing, strengthen the societal
bonds that lie at the heart of Western liberal, democratic traditions.
If undermined by unsound money and inflation, these traditions are
at risk of being displaced by authoritarian ones instead. As I am an
optimist in this regard, in my view the present, elevated level of
global monetary instability represents golden writing on the wall.

Further Reading

Articles

Barro, Robert J. "Money and the Price Level under the Gold Standard." *Economic Journal* 89 (March 1979).

Barro, Robert J., and David B. Gordon. "A Positive Theory of Monetary Policy in a Natural Rate Model." *Journal of Political Economy* 91 (August 1983).

Bordo, Michael D., and Lars Jonung. "A Return to the Convertibility Principle? Monetary and Fiscal Regimes in International Perspective." (November 2000). Paper prepared for the International Economic Association conference in Trento, Italy, September 4–7, 1997. Online: http://swopec.hhs.se/hastef/papers/hastef0415.pdf.

Bordo, M.D., and F.E. Kydland. "The Gold Standard as a Rule: An Essay in Exploration." *Explorations in Economic History* 32 (1995): 423–464.

Bordo, M.D., and H. Rockoff. "The Gold Standard as a 'Good Housekeeping Seal of Approval.'" *Journal of Economic History* 56 (1996).

Crafts, N., and P. Fearon. "Lessons from the 1930s' Great Depression." *Oxford Review of Economic Policy* 26 (2010): 285–317.

Davidson, Laura F. "The Causes of Price Inflation and Deflation: Fundamental Economic Principles the Deflationists Have Ignored." *Libertarian Papers* 3, art. 13 (2011).

"Dollars, Deficits and the International Monetary System." *Review of the Federal Reserve Bank of St. Louis*, July 1971.

Eichengreen, Barry. "The Dollar Dilemma." *Foreign Affairs*, September/October 2009. Council on Foreign Relations. Online: www.foreignaffairs.com/articles/65241/barry-eichengreen/the-dollar-dilemma.

Eichengreen, Barry, and Michael Bordo. "Crises Now and Then: What Lessons from the Last Era of Financial Globalization?" National Bureau of Economic Research Working Paper 8716 (January 2002).

Eichengreen, B., and R. Portes. "Debt and Default in the 1930s: Causes and Consequences." *European Economic Review* 30 (1986): 599–640.

Farchy, Jack. "Dollar Seen to Lose Its Reserve Currency Status." *Financial Times*, June 27, 2011.

Flandreau, Marc, and Mathilde Maurel. "Monetary Union, Trade Integration, and Business Cycles in the 19th Century." *Open Economies Review* 16 (2005): 135–152.

Frankel, Jeffrey. "The Effect of Monetary Policy on Real Commodity Prices." In John Campbell, ed., *Asset Prices and Monetary Policy*, Chicago: University of Chicago Press, 2008.

Frankel, Jeffrey. "Peg the Export Price Index: A Proposed Monetary Regime for Small Countries." *Journal of Policy Modelling*, June 2005.

Friedman, Milton. "Commodity-Reserve Currency." *Journal of Political Economy* 59 (June 1951).

Friedman, Milton. "The Resource Cost of Irredeemable Paper Money." *Journal of Political Economy* 94 (June 1986).

Gallarotti, Giulio M. "The Rise of the Classical Gold Standard: The Role of Focal Points and Synergistic Effects in Spontaneous Order." *Humane Studies Review* (2001).

Herbener, Jeffrey M. "After the Age of Inflation: Austrian Proposals for Monetary Reform." *Quarterly Journal of Austrian Economics* 5, no. 4 (Winter 2002).

Kydland, Finn, and Edward C. Prescott. "Rules Rather than Discretion: The Inconsistency of Optimal Plans." *Journal of Political Economy* 85 (June 1977).

Laffer, Arthur B., and Charles W. Kadlec. "The Point of Linking the Dollar to Gold." *Wall Street Journal*, October 13, 1982.

McCallum, Bennett T. "Alternative Monetary Policy Rules: A Comparison with Historical Settings for the United States, the United Kingdom, and Japan." *Federal Reserve Bank of Richmond Economic Quarterly* 86 (Winter 2000).

McCallum, Bennett T. "Robustness Properties of a Rule for Monetary Policy." *Carnegie-Rochester Conference Series for Public Policy* 29 (Autumn 1988).

McKinnon, R. "The Rules of the Game: International Money in Historical Perspective." *Journal of Economic Literature* 31 (1993): 1–44.

Meissner, C.H. "A New World Order: Explaining the Diffusion of the Classical Gold Standard." National Bureau of Economic Research Working Paper 9233, September 2002.

Meissner, M. Christopher, and J. Ernesto López-Córdova. "Exchange-Rate Regimes and International Trade: Evidence from the Classical Gold Standard Era." *American Economic Review* 93, no. 1 (March 2003): 344–353.

Modigliani, F. and M. Miller. "The Cost of Capital, Corporation Finance and the Theory of Investment." *American Economic Review* 48, no. 3 (June 1958): 261–297.

Morys, Matthias. "The Emergence of the Classical Gold Standard." Economic History Society Annual Conference, Exeter (March 2007).

Mundell, Robert M. "Gold Would Serve into the 21st Century." *Wall Street Journal*, September 30, 1981.

Obstfeld, Maurice, and Alan M. Taylor. "Soverign Risk, Credibility and the Gold Standard: 1870–1913 versus 1925–1931." National Bureau of Economic Research Working Paper 9345 (2002).

Ohanian, Lee. "What, or Who, Started the Great Depression?" *Journal of Economic Theory* 144, no. 6 (November 2009).

Ohanian, Lee, and Harold Cole. "Stimulus and the Depression: The Untold Story." *Wall Street Journal*, September 26, 2011.

Reinhart, Carmen, and Belen Sbrancia. "The Liquidation of Government Debt." NBER Working Paper 16893 (2011).

"Reserve Accumulation and International Monetary Stability." International Monetary Fund Working Paper, Strategy Policy and Review Department, April 13, 2010.

Romer, Paul. "Increasing Returns and Long Run Growth." *Journal of Political Economy* 94, 1002–1037, 1986.

Salerno, Joseph T. "The Gold Standard: An Analysis of Some Recent Proposals." *CATO Policy Analysis* 16, September 9, 1982.

Sargent, T., and N. Wallace. "Rational Expectations, the Optimal Monetary Instrument and the Optimal Money Supply Rule." *Journal of Political Economy* 83, no. 2 (April 1975).

Schularick, M., and T. Steger. "International Financial Integration and Economic Growth—New Evidence from the First Era of Financial Globalization." Center for Economic and Policy Research.

Selgin, George, and Lawrence H. White. "Credible Currency: A Constitutional Perspective." *Constitutional Political Economy* 16 (March 2005).

Taylor, John. "Discretion versus Policy Rules in Practice." Carnegie-Rochester Conference Series on Public Policy 39 (December 1993).

Taylor, John. "Monetary Policy During a Transition to Rational Expectation." *Journal of Political Economy* 83, no. 5 (October 1975).

Wanniski, Jude. "A Job Only Gold Can Do." *New York Times*, August 27, 1981.

White, Lawrence H. "Is the Gold Standard Still the Gold Standard among Monetary Systems?" *CATO Briefing Papers* 100 (February 8, 2008).

Wolf, N. "Europe's Great Depression: Coordination Failure after the First World War." *Oxford Review of Economic Policy* 26 (2010): 339–369.

Books

Akerlof, George A., and Robert J. Shiller. *Animal Spirits: How Human Psychology Drives the Economy, and Why It Matters for Global Capitalism*. Princeton, NJ: Princeton University Press, 2009.

Arthur, Brian W., John Holland, Blake LeBaron, and Richard Palmer. *The Economy as an Evolving Complex System II.* Brian Arthur, Steven Durlaf, and David Lane, eds. Menlo Park: Addison-Wesley, 1997.

Bayoumi, T., B. Eichengreen, and M.P. Taylor, eds. *Modern Perspectives on the Gold Standard.* Cambridge University Press, 1996.

Bernstein, Peter. *Capital Ideas Evolving.* Hoboken, NJ: John Wiley & Sons, 2007.

Bordo, M., and B. Eichengreen, eds. *A Retrospective on the Bretton Woods System.* Chicago: University of Chicago Press, 1993.

Brandeis, Louis. *Other People's Money—And How the Bankers Use It.* 1914. Reprint by BiblioLife, 2009.

Bresciani-Tirroni, Constantino. *The Economics of Inflation.* London: George Allen & Unwin, 1937.

Cochran, P. John, and R. Fred Glahe. *The Hayek-Keynes Debate—Lessons for Current Business Cycle Research.* Edwin Mellen Press, 1999.

Dorn, A. James, and J. Anna Schwartz, eds. *The Search for Stable Money: Essays on Monetary Reform.* Chicago: University of Chicago Press and the Cato Institute, 1987.

Ebeling, M. Richard, ed. *The Austrian Theory of the Trade Cycle and Other Essays.* Ludwig Von Mises Institute, 1996.

Eichengreen, Barry. *Exorbitant Privilege.* Oxford University Press, 2011.

Eichengreen, Barry, and M. Flandreau, eds. *The Gold Standard in Theory and History,* 2nd ed. Routledge, 1997.

Friedman, Milton, and Anna Schwartz. *A Monetary History of the United States, 1867–1960.* Princeton, NJ: Princeton University Press, 1963.

Garet, Garrett. *The Bubble That Broke the World.* Boston: Little, Brown, & Company, 1932. Auburn, AL: Ludwig von Mises Institute, 2007.

Garrison, Roger. *Time and Money: The Macroeconomics of Capital Structure.* Routledge, 2001.

Geisst, Charles R. *Wall Street: A History: From Its Beginnings to the Fall of Enron.* Oxford University Press, 2004.

Gouge, William M. *A Short History of Paper Money and Banking.* Auburn, AL: Ludwig von Mises Institute, n.d. Orig. pub. 1835.

Guindley, Guillaume. *The International Money Triangle: Myths and Realities.* Trans. Michael L. Hoffman. White Plains, NY: ME Sharpe, 1977.

Hayek, F.A. *Denationalisation of Money: The Argument Refined.* Institute of Economic Affairs, 1990. Auburn, AL: Ludwig von Mises Institute, 2009.

Hayek, F.A. *The Fatal Conceit: The Errors of Socialism.* University of Chicago Press, 1988.

Hazlitt, Henry, ed. *The Critics of Keynesian Economics.* Princeton, NJ: D. Van Nostrand Co., 1960.

Hazlitt, Henry. *Economics in One Lesson.* New York: Harper & Brothers, 1946.

Hazlitt, Henry. *From Bretton Woods to World Inflation: A Study of Causes and Consequences.* Regnery Gateway, 1984. Auburn, AL: Ludwig Von Mises Institute, 2008.

Hazlitt, Henry. *The Inflation Crisis and How to Resolve It.* Auburn, AL: Ludwig von Mises Institute, 2009.

Hazlitt, Henry. *What You Should Know about Inflation.* Princeton, NJ: D. Van Nostrand Company, 1964.

Heilbroner, Robert. *The Worldly Philosophers: The Lives, Times and Ideas of the Great Economic Thinkers.* New York: Simon & Schuster, 1953.

Higgs, Robert. *Crisis and Leviathan: Critical Episodes in the Growth of American Government.* Oxford University Press and the Pacific Research Institute for Public Policy, 1987.

Huerta De Soto, Jesus. *Money, Bank Credit and Economic Cycles.* Auburn, AL: Ludwig von Mises Institute, 2006.

Issing, Otmar, Vitor Gaspar, Ignazio Angeloni, and Oreste Tristani. *Monetary Policy in the Euro Area.* Cambridge University Press, 2001.

Jastram, W. Roy, with updated material by Jill Leyland. *The Golden Constant.* Edward Elgar Pub., 2009.

Kindleberger, Charles P. *Manias, Panics, and Crashes: A History of Financial Crises.* 4th ed. New York: John Wiley & Sons, 2000.

Lehrman, Lewis R. *A Monetary Reform Plan without Official Reserve Currencies: How We Get from There to Here.* Lehrman Institute, 2011.

Lewis, Hunter. *Where Keynes Went Wrong.* Axios, 2009.

Lindberg, Leon N., and Charles S. Maier, eds. *The Politics of Inflation of Economic Stagnation.* Washington DC: Brookings Institution, 1985.

Litan, Robert. *What Should Banks Do?* Washington DC: Brookings Institution, 1987.

Lowenstein, Roger. *When Genius Failed.* New York: Random House, 2000.

Mandelbrot, Benoit. *The (Mis)Behavior of Markets: A Fractal View of Financial Turbulence.* New York: Basic Books, 2004.

Markopolos, Harry. *No One Would Listen: A True Financial Thriller.* Hoboken, NJ: John Wiley & Sons, 2010.

Markowitz, Harry M. *Portfolio Selection: Efficient Diversification of Investments.* New York: John Wiley & Sons, 1959.

McCloskey, Donald. N. *If You're So Smart: The Narrative of Economic Expertise.* Chicago: University of Chicago Press, 1990.

Melzer, Allan. *A History of the Federal Reserve.* Vol. 2, book 2, *1970–1986.* Chicago: University of Chicago Press, 2010.

Mises, Ludwig von. *Economic Policy: Thoughts for Today and Tomorrow.* Auburn, AL: Ludwig von Mises Institute, 2006.

Mises, Ludwig von. *Human Action.* New Haven: Yale University Press, 1949.

Mises, Ludwig von. *The Theory of Money and Credit.* Trans. H.E. Baston. New Haven: Yale University Press, 1953.

Murphy, P. Robert. *The Politically Incorrect Guide to Capitalism.* Regnery, 2007.

Murphy, P. Robert. *The Politically Incorrect Guide to the Great Depression and the New Deal.* Regnery, 2009.

Obstfeld, M., and A.M. Taylor. *Global Capital Markets: Integration, Crisis, Growth.* Cambridge University Press, 2004.

Odell, John S. *U.S. International Monetary Policy: Markets, Power and Ideas as Sources of Change.* Princeton NJ: Princeton University Press, 1982.

Powell, Jim. *FDR's Folly: How Roosevelt and His New Deal Prolonged the Great Depression.* Three Rivers Press, 2003.

Reinhart, Carmen M., and Kenneth S. Rogoff. *This Time Is Different: Eight Centuries of Financial Folly.* Princeton, NJ: Princeton University Press, 2009.

Reisman, George. *Capitalism: A Treatise on Economics.* Ottawa, IL: Jameson Books, 1996.

Rickards, James. *Currency Wars: The Making of the Next Global Crisis.* New York: Portfolio/Penguin, 2011.

Rizzo, Mario, and Lawrence White. *Foundations of the Market Economy.* Routledge.

Rothbard, Murray N. *America's Great Depression.* Auburn, AL: Ludwig Von Mises Institute, 2000.

Rothbard, Murray N. *The Case against the Fed.* Auburn, AL: Ludwig von Mises Institute, 1994.

Rothbard, Murray N. *The Case for a 100% Gold Dollar.* Auburn, AL: Ludwig Von Mises Institute, 2005.

Rothbard, Murray N. *A History of Money and Banking in the United States: The Colonial Era to World War II.* Auburn, AL: Ludwig von Mises Institute, 2005.

Rothbard, Murray N. *The Mystery of Banking.* Auburn, AL: Ludwig von Mises Institute, 2008.

Rothbard, Murray N. *The Panic of 1819.* Auburn, AL: Ludwig von Mises Institute, 2007.

Rothbard, Murray N. *What Has Government Done to Our Money?* Auburn, AL: Ludwig von Mises Institute, 2005.

Rueff, Jacques. *The Age of Inflation.* Trans. Roger Glemet. New York: Macmillan, 1964.

Rueff, Jacques. *The Monetary Sin of the West.* Trans. Roger Glemet. New York: Macmillan, 1972.

Salerno, Joseph T. *Money, Sound and Unsound.* Auburn, AL: Ludwig von Mises Institute, 2010.

Samuelson, Paul, and William Nordhaus. *Economics.* New York: McGraw-Hill, 2009; first published 1948.

Sargent, J. Thomas. *Rational Expectations and Inflation.* New York: Harper & Row, 1986.

Scammell, W.M. *International Monetary Policy: Bretton Woods and After.* New York: John Wiley & Sons, 1975.

Schumpeter, Joseph. *Capitalism, Socialism, and Democracy.* New York: Harper & Row, 1950.

Senholz, F. Hans. *Age of Inflation.* Western Islands, 1979.

Selgin, George A. *Less Than Zero: The Case for a Falling Price Level in a Growing Economy.* London: Institute for Economic Affairs, 1997.

Selgin, George A. *The Theory of Free Banking: Money Supply under Competitive Note Issue.* Rowman & Littlefield, 1988.

Shelton, Judy. *A Guide to Sound Money.* Washington, DC: Atlas Economic Research Foundation, 2010.

Shiller, Robert. *Irrational Exuberance.* Princeton, NJ: Princeton University Press, 2000.

Smith, Adam. *An Inquiry into the Nature and Causes of the Wealth of Nations.* Ed. Kathryn Sutherland. Oxford: Oxford University Press, 1998.

Sornette, Didier. *Why Stock Markets Crash: Critical Events in Complex Financial Systems.* Princeton, NJ: Princeton University Press, 2003.

Sylla, Richard, and Sidney Homer. *A History of Interest Rates.* 4th ed. Hoboken, NJ: John Wiley & Sons, 2005.

Studenski, Paul, and Herman Edward *Krooss. Financial History of the United States.* New York: McGraw-Hill, 1952.

Treaster, Joseph B. *Paul Volcker: The Making of a Financial Legend.* Hoboken, NJ: John Wiley & Sons, 2004.

White, H. Lawrence. *Competition and Currency: Essays on Free Banking and Money.* New York: New York University Press, 1989.

About the Author

JOHN BUTLER worked for over 15 years as an interest rate, foreign exchange, and commodity strategist at major banks around the world before setting up his own, independent investment firm in London in 2010, where he serves as the Chief Investment Officer. He has written extensively on financial topics and has been quoted in the *Financial Times*, *The Wall Street Journal*, and the *Frankfurter Allgemeine Zeitung*, among other publications. He is the author and publisher of the popular *Amphora Report* newsletter, posted regularly to a handful of prominent financial websites, and is an occasional speaker at global investment conferences. He resides in the English countryside with his wife and four children.

Index